The Civilian Conservation Corps and the Construction of the Virginia Kendall Reserve, 1933–1939

CCC workers at Virginia Kendall Reserve laying locally hewn stone for steps in the Ledges area, no date (National Park Service)

The

Civilian Conservation Corps

and the

Construction of the

Virginia Kendall Reserve,

1933–1939

EDITED BY KENNETH J. BINDAS

Published in cooperation with the National Park Service and Eastern National

The Kent State University Press

KENT, OHIO

Frontis: CCC statue in front of Happy Days visitor center
(photo by Marina Vladova)

© 2013 by The Kent State University Press, Kent, Ohio 44242
All rights reserved
ISBN 978-1-60635-155-0
Manufactured in the United States of America

Publication of this book is made possible in part through the generous
support of the National Park Service and Eastern National.

Cataloging information for this title is available at the Library of Congress.

Contents

Hiking to the Ledges from Happy Days (photo by Marina Vladova)

Entering the Reserve

KENNETH J. BINDAS

As you're driving up Truxell Road from Akron Peninsula Road or down Ohio Route 303 from Route 8, you cannot escape the natural beauty of the fields, the trees with their full canopies spreading green across the blue and white of the sky, the growing quiet. Or, maybe you've parked your car and begun your hike around the Ledges area, or around Virginia Kendall Lake; very quickly you find yourself in nature, away from the sounds and experiences of the outside world. You are in a special, natural space that seems to transcend time and place. Nature grounds our senses and reminds us, in the largest sense, of where we have come from; in the smallest, it takes us from where we are today. At least, this is the feeling I get when I'm driving to or hiking around the Cuyahoga Valley National Park's Virginia Kendall Reserve. The sights, sounds, and sensations of the area seem to burst with stories.

This work tells one such story. It details how the Virginia Kendall Reserve, this beautiful natural area, came to be, for it wasn't always what it is today. More than 65,000 years ago, as the Wisconsin glacier made its slow retreat north through western Ohio, it created a series of lakes. As the modern form of the Great Lakes took shape, some of the smaller lakes, like Lake Cuyahoga, receded to form creeks and rivers, carving pathways and breaking the land from swamps to flood plains and valleys. Around 12,000 years ago, the "Ka-ih-ogh-ha" river, as Native Americans thousands of years later called it, took its modern form. The crooked river began its roughly one-hundred-mile, U-shaped journey in modern-day Geauga County, flowing south before sharply turning north in Summit County, carving out a path through what became known as the Cuyahoga Valley, and then emptying into Lake Erie in Cleveland. Adena and Hopewell native cultures had utilized the lower portions of the river, but for the most part, migration and use of the area was limited due to the fervent swamps along the shore, the steep slopes and poor soil of the river valley, and the river's lack of navigability. Before Europeans came to the area, natives followed and traversed the river, marking it as a portage between lands to the east and those less hospitable in the west. The land in and around the Cuyahoga Valley was acquired by the United States through several treaties between 1785–1805, but settlement was slow.

The Cuyahoga Valley represented both splendor and a challenge for those who came to settle; on one hand, marvelous in its beauty, on the other, a barrier to settlement and trade. And, in the early nineteenth century, unspoiled nature was valued not for its beauty but for what it could bring forth—crops, cattle, and security. To get around the inconvenience of the land and river, Ohioans first built the Ohio-Erie Canal, then the Valley Railway, and, in the twentieth-century, roads for automobiles, all of which followed the Cuyahoga River and its valley. Settlers used this land to raise cattle or crops, selling to burgeoning local Cleveland and Akron markets. As these cities boomed and wages in factories outstripped the profits from working the land, fewer people farmed the valley. Around this time, in 1913, Heyward Kendall, a young man working for his father's Cleveland insurance company, bought fifteen acres of land from the Ritchie family, who had raised cattle on it. Eventually, he would purchase the 430 acres that came to be the Kendall Reserve, building a small cabin on the land where he and his friends would spend the weekends. The story of the Virginia Kendall Reserve and the role the Civilian Conservation Corp played, the focus of this book, begins with his death in 1927.[1]

The inspiration for this study of how the Virginia Kendall Reserve (Kendall Reserve) was made, for what purpose, and whom it served came from several fronts. On a personal level, my daughter Savannah and I used to go to an area within the Kendall Reserve called "the

Ledges," the first area purchased by Hayward, where she relished hiking the trails around the giant sandstone outcroppings. Sometimes she liked to bring her brothers—Zachary and Colin—to show them how cool the area was. She told me once, as we rounded the bend to Ice Box Cave, that coming around that bend was like going back in time and that it felt exciting just being there. And, judging by the number of people of all ages hiking this area, viewing those rocks, and looking just as in awe as I still am when I go there with my family Sadie, Faye, and wife Marina, many people feel these same sensations—perhaps it's the history—of the area. This mystique and attraction are also felt when walking around Virginia Kendall Lake, or hiking down the hill and stumbling upon the Octagon Pavilion, or coming out from the tunnel under Route 303 onto the majesty of the Happy Days visitor center. There is simply something about the Kendall Reserve that attracts visitors. Maybe it's the peaceful feeling, the calm and cool of the rocks and water. I can't seem to pinpoint what it is, but I return again and again to experience it.

Cross-country skiing around Kendall Lake (photo by Marina Vladova)

My personal enjoyment of the area intersected with my professional interests as a Depression-era historian and teacher at Kent State
University. My first reaction to the Virginia Kendall Reserve was not
unlike what most people experience when they enter any natural area,
for I assumed that it had always been like this, or at least since the
days of the early Republic. The Kendall Reserve has an ancient feel.
As an historian, I began to ask questions about the park, primarily
of a National Park Service employee named Jeff Winstel, who told
me about the acquisition of the land, how it came to be a park, and
who "created" it.

The part of his story that most caught my ear concerned the Civilian
Conservation Corps (CCC) and how this collection of young men had
come to the reserve in 1933 and remade the area. This spurred more
professional interest, and I began researching the creation of the Kendall Reserve and asking other questions regarding its connection to the
1930s and the CCC. All of this led to a course I taught in the fall of 2009
entitled "The American Reformation: The Depression Era." Nineteen
students enrolled, made up of master's-level graduate students and
interested and motivated upper-level undergraduates, and I decided
to use the Kendall Reserve and the CCC as part of a project-based research practicum for the students. I wanted them to apply what they
were reading in the assigned secondary sources, hearing in lectures
and media presentations, and discussing with each other in group
presentations. More than anything else, I wanted to teach them basic
historical methodology, how to write history and learn from each other
as they did it. This meant creating a project with the real prospect of
publication. I had already collected and distributed to them much of the
primary research, made up of government and archival records, case
studies, National Park Service reports, and even a few oral histories. I
also pointed them in the direction of other usable sources. I designed
the course lectures and readings to dovetail with their research on the
reserve and its larger contextual meaning within the Depression era.
We visited the area together, and most of them returned regularly to
get a feel for the place. And finally, as a carrot of sorts, I told them that
I would incorporate the best research papers with my own writing and
try to get our work published as a team project.

*The Civilian Conservation Corps and the Construction of the Virginia
Kendall Reserve, 1933–1939* is the result of this adventure. All the

Facing page: Fall trail near the Ledges (photo by Marina Vladova)

students who stayed in the class—Serene Artino, Charles Bromley, David Busch, Courtney Cates, Jordan Cormier, Amanda Ebersol, Andrea Hauser, Charles May, Sarah Reichenbach, Colleen Benoit, John Brace, Lindsey Calderwood, Meredith Soeder, Michele Curran, Kristen Ellis, Stephanie Vincent, and Felicia Wetzig—did excellent work throughout the semester. Those students whose papers went above and beyond expectations came to be part of this book. I cut, pasted, edited, moved, created new text, and blended their stories into sections of a chapter I was writing for a larger monograph, and, along with Associate Editor Meredith Soeder, tried to weave a portrait of the Virginia Kendall Reserve that helps to explain why it is what it is. We secured photographs from the Cuyahoga Valley National Park Service and received a vast amount of help from the staff, including Anthony Gareau, Jennie Vasarhelyi, Melissa Arnold, Arrye Rosser, and Lynette Sprague-Falk. The contemporary photographs were taken by Marina Vladova (special thanks to Amelia R. Masten for digital processing) and are meant to convey what resulted from the vision, commitment, and hard work in the early part of the last century. The maps were created by Jason Haley. *The Civilian Conservation Corps and the Construction of the Virginia Kendall Reserve, 1933–1939* began as an adventure with family and continues. I welcome you to join in by writing in the margins of the book about what you've read, going to the reserve,

Visitors' names carved on trees (photo by Marina Vladova)

and seeing how it feels to know how and why the Virginia Kendall Reserve came about. I encourage your comments, suggestions, and photographs—go to our Facebook page, CCC and VKR, and become part of this ongoing story. Your experience is what makes the Virginia Kendall Reserve so special, and we hope that what we have presented here will somehow make the experience even better.

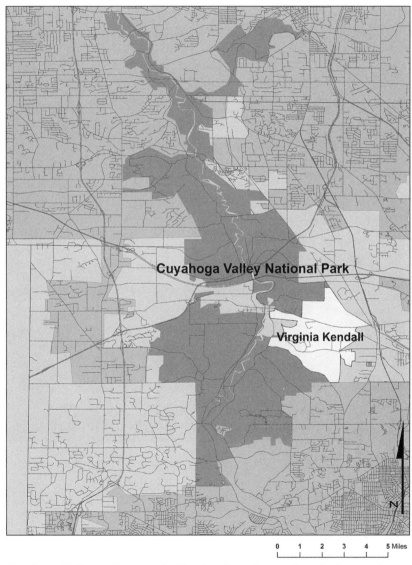

Cuyahoga Valley National Park, Cleveland is to the north and Akron to the south (map by Jason Haley)

Park Policeman Howard Dittoe in front of CCC sign, no date (National Park Service)

1

The CCC Comes to Virginia Kendall Reserve

KENNETH J. BINDAS, DAVID BUSCH, STEPHANIE VINCENT,
AND COLLEEN BENOIT

On April 5, 1939, Leonard Tulloch had just finished another long day of work with the Civilian Conservation Corps. He sat down on his bunk, tuned the radio to WADC, a local Akron station, and heard the broadcaster's booming voice announce, "This station is pleased to relinquish the next 15 minutes to the Civilian Conservation Corps." Tulloch leaned back onto his dusty but comfortable cot, flipped off his muddy shoes, and listened to Harold S. Wagner, the president of the American Institute of Park Executives and the person responsible for bringing the CCC to the Cuyahoga Valley. Tulloch could picture that hard-nosed Dutchman leaning forward in his chair, preaching the good news of the CCC in Ohio. "It is scarcely necessary for me to remind my radio audience of the improvements that the Corps has brought about Kendall Park," Wagner began, "It is a fact, however, that practically all of the features that have been fitted into that area were carried out by the CCC. The lake and its bath house and winter sports facilities; the picnic areas and play space; the shelters and water supply system, and the well-hidden trails and ample roadways and parking spaces were all boy-built." Tulloch nodded his head in approval, especially about the line "boy-built." This "is reason enough," Wagner continued, "for us to be everlastingly grateful to the CCC."[1]

Harold Wagner, no date
(National Park Service)

The relationship between Tulloch and Wagner rested on more than just the CCC, for both were instrumental in creating the wonderful landscape that is the Virginia Kendall Reserve. When President Franklin D. Roosevelt issued Executive Order #6101 on April 5, 1933, to create what was officially to become the CCC, coming on the heels of congressional passage of the Emergency Relief Appropriation Act on March 31, then Director-Secretary of the Akron Metropolitan Park District Harold S. Wagner immediately began planning how to make use of this seminal opportunity in northeastern Ohio. One of his first locations involved the recently acquired Kendall Reserve. He saw the area as the perfect place, between metropolitan Cleveland and Akron, to expose people to nature and provide a place to hike the rolling hills, scale the ledges, picnic in the fields, swim in the lake that would be constructed, and simply enjoy the beauty of the natural environment.

Wagner sent a proposal to Washington, D.C., for a CCC camp at the Kendall Reserve in August 1933, and by the start of the new year, the first recruits began to trickle in. Tulloch was among them, and for him, the Kendall Reserve meant work and a life-changing experience.[2]

When, in the spring of 1933, President Roosevelt signed the bill that created the Civilian Conservation Corps into law, few people foresaw its long-term significance. But Congress renewed the program in 1935 and again in 1937, and only dismantled it in late December 1941, with the official end date of July 2, 1942. On the same day he announced the creation of the CCC, FDR appointed Robert Fechner its director. Fechner remained in the post until his death in 1939. During his term, Fechner steered the CCC clear of the congressional and public scrutiny that plagued many other New Deal programs.

He did this by reinforcing the CCC's positive contributions to the enrollees, their families, communities, and the country. In order to make the CCC work, Fechner had to negotiate the multivariate interests of representatives from the departments of Labor, Interior, Agriculture, and War that made up his advisory boards, as well as of all the agencies under each of their authority. The Department of Labor, for example, was responsible for junior enrollee selection; the Veterans' Administration for veteran enrollees; the War Department for physical examinations, enrollment, transportation, organization, and conditioning of the enrollees; the specific work projects fell under the command of the Agriculture Department; and the Department of the Interior dealt with the planning and supervision of the work.[3]

The CCC was initially designed to accommodate about twelve thousand men (women were not allowed into the Corps), but by the summer of 1933 more states had requested CCC activities, so that by early July, three hundred thousand young men, veterans, and local experienced men (LEM) had enrolled. The basic recruit earned thirty dollars a month, of which twenty-five went back to his family. During that first crucial year, when all concerned were uncertain as to whether the CCC would succeed and what it would actually do, the physical results were, according to Fechner, "remarkable." First, the infrastructure for further development was laid, with construction of more than 25,000 miles of truck trails and 15,000 miles of telephone lines to enable the development of work camps in national and state forests and parks. After laying this foundation, actual work in these areas included insect and disease control on more than three million acres of land, the planting of ninety-eight million seedlings, and fire-fighting equal to 678,000 man-days. But even more significant, Fechner wrote, was that the CCC helped nearly three hundred thousand young men overcome "spiritual and physical depression" by teaching the values of cooperation, hard-work, and a "healthful environment."[4]

Aside from the social and natural contributions, the sheer size of the CCC and its impact encouraged states and local areas to get involved. According to the 1938 *Annual Report,* the CCC's roughly 273,000 men consumed 12,455,600 pounds of bacon, 62,278,100 pounds of beef, 12,455,600 pounds of chicken, 99,645,000 eggs, 62,278,100 pounds of potatoes, 27,679,100 pounds of pork, 31,133,500 pounds of sugar, 74,733,750 pounds of flour, and 12,455,600 pounds of coffee. All of this translates into 1,736,560 hogs, 103,800 steers, 3,113,906 chickens, tens of millions of acres of land for wheat, potatoes, sugar cane, beans, and the astounding number of other commodities necessary to provide more than 298,935,000 meals for the recruits at a cost of $159.40 per man for the year. To clothe the men and provide them with bed linens added another nineteen million dollars to the CCC budget that year. These commodities—not including wages, transportation costs, and other incidentals—were often locally produced and thus provided a tremendous boon to economies across the nation. Local and state representatives were quick to recognize the multiple ways in which a CCC camp might help to alleviate unemployment and stimulate local business and industry, and so they sought to create projects.[5]

In order to accommodate these requests and to streamline the approval process, the CCC was divided into nine Corps areas. Each had a central administrative location that processed camp requests, oversaw design and work assignments, and wrote quarterly and yearly reports to be included in Fechner's *Annual Report.* Each Corps area had as its anchor a state with a higher number of recruits in order to even

Tree planting at VKR, no date (National Park Service)

out the regional distribution of federal monies and to target those areas with the highest employment need and service activities. While Pennsylvania, for example, in the third area, had large enrollment numbers due to its high unemployment rate, many of the recruits were sent to the fourth (southern states, excluding Texas) and ninth (Rocky Mountain west) areas. This meant that the twenty-five dollars of an enrollee's monthly paycheck that went back to the home state would benefit the other areas that procured supplies necessary to operate the camps locally. Ohio served as the anchor for the fifth area, which also included West Virginia, Indiana, and Kentucky, and while many recruits were also sent to the south and west, many more remained in the state.

Ohio was particularly hard hit by the economic collapse, as its economy focused on manufacturing and farming, two areas that were among the most depressed when FDR took office. For example, more than forty percent of factory workers and sixty-seven percent of construction workers were unemployed by the time of the CCC's creation, and in urban areas like Cleveland, Youngstown, Akron, and Toledo, the overall unemployment rate ran between fifty and eighty percent. Overall, the state's unemployment rate held steady at thirty-seven percent in early 1933, with rates much higher for those between the ages of sixteen and twenty-five, the target ages of the CCC. That the CCC focused on young people is understandable when looking at the continued unemployment problem this group faced. For example, in 1937, when the overall unemployment rate hovered near sixteen percent nationally, the rate for young people stood closer to thirty-eight percent, and in Ohio's urban areas, this number was much higher. There was real concern throughout the state and the nation that a whole generation of young people might be condemned to a life of under- or unemployment and fall through the cracks in the American dream.

One of the central charges of the CCC in Ohio was to both employ young men and provide a meaning for their citizenship. Given the realities of the unemployment problem for young people in the Depression, the administration felt it important to use the CCC to help assure them of their positive role in society, thereby building their sense of commitment to the nation. And, as a state hard hit by the depression, Ohio went all out, and by the end of the CCC's first year, it boasted forty-one camps scattered throughout the state, a number that grew to fifty-one by 1936, employing an average of 6,624 men. Another 3,951 men on the state's rolls were sent to other areas for work. The work accomplished by the Ohio CCC in 1938 alone included building dozens of latrines, cabins, lodges, miles of fences, stone walls, seeding, sodding, ditch diversion, bank sloping, stream and lake protection, trails, planting more than 29,000 trees, and countless other tasks from stocking lakes with fish to mosquito control.[6]

The CCC focused on essentially two ideas—employing the millions of young men who otherwise had little chance of employment and remaking and reclaiming natural areas—both of which problems predated the Depression. The rapid industrial and urban growth leading up to the 1930s had not only resulted in a host of social problems for the nation's youth, but a separation from the collective past. An organization like the CCC could, as Arthur Dunham wrote in *The Survey* in May 1933, serve as the "rallying of the American pioneer spirit in the advance . . . [of] the next chapter of our national life." Thus, the intersection of practical need and what Roosevelt saw as "the moral and spiritual value of such work" underscored the role and influence of modernist ideas within his administration and set the tone for the social and cultural reformation that reached its apex during the Depression era. Key to this process was the incorporation of experts like

Constructing the bathhouse, 1936 (National Park Service)

Kendall Lake bathhouse today, lake view (photo by Marina Vladova)

landscape architects into the planning, design, and oversight of the areas under CCC authority to help transform, according to historian Phoebe Cutler, "what had been largely a creature of chance into a synthesis of orderly design." While modern-day environmental policy leans more toward preservation, Wagner's focus, given the reserve's previous usage to farm corn and as a dairy, leaned more toward land reclamation for both recreation and preservation purposes. He saw his role not in the terms of modern ecologists, but as a land management specialist. He was like others in charge of local CCC projects, who sought balance between the recreational needs of the people and the desire to preserve or at least maintain some aspect of wilderness. They applied this policy throughout the country, hoping to achieve what Wagner hoped to do in the Kendall Reserve, namely transform an un-developed and abandoned area into one "designed . . . to choreograph visitors' experiences . . . [and encourage] the aesthetic appreciation of landscapes and allow the spiritual communion with nature."[7]

The organizers of the CCC, primarily the Department of the Interior and the National Park Service, in cooperation with the many state-level directors and local project coordinators, wanted to make nature more useful, functional, and to a large extent, consumable. Given their generational cohort—born and educated in an era of rampant industrialism, urbanism, associated with capitalism—they saw nature as something untamed, wild, and therefore not very useful. In order to make these natural areas socially functional, either for the people to experience or for industry to utilize, they needed to be made modern, controlled, designed, and authentic. This may sound strange to our modern ears, but in that era, with the training and education provided at the most prestigious universities endorsing land management techniques, those in charge of the CCC believed nature needed to be made more "natural" than its wild state. Parks at the national, state, and municipal level needed to be made more accessible and the president hoped that the CCC's work would go a long way to developing these resources.

Fanning Hearon of the National Park Service (NPS) paid homage to the CCC's work in 1935 not only for saving trees and helping unemployed youth, but for making the parks assessable to the public in the form of "lakes and cabins and trails to the peaks" while leaving the bulk of the wildlife areas "untouched so this scenic beauty... may go on unmolested." The NPS saw its effort as part of a new world in which the science of the day and the application of reason allowed a unique

CCC work crews at VKR, no date (National Park Service)

opportunity to remake nature as socially useful and functional. Theirs was no utopian agenda, but a practical, logical, reasonable reformation of the role and place of nature in the new consciousness taking hold during the Depression era. "Our forests," Roosevelt wrote in 1937, "have been and continue to be a part of the basic pattern woven into our national fabric [and the CCC] . . . is helping to rebuild our youth as well as our forest resources," shaping the future for both.[8]

Roosevelt's commitment to nature began in his youth and continued throughout his political career. In 1891, a young and vivacious FDR explored the German countryside on a trip with his family. An expansive forest on the edge of one of the towns there intrigued the young man not only for its beauty, but because the human maintenance and oversight of the forest financially supported the town. To FDR the forest was both spiritually enlightening and economically pragmatic. This simple experience laid the foundation of what would become Roosevelt's conservationist and environmental world view. When he took over his family's Hyde Park estate in 1910, Roosevelt, according to historian A. L. Owen, "pioneered in farm forestry and showed his Hudson Valley neighbors how their land could be used wisely and profitably." Coming of age as a politician during the early part of the last century, Gifford Pinchot's views on the environment were pervasive and influenced Roosevelt. Pinchot's central tenet was "the adjustment of one forest to another so that the net public benefit would result—to obtain the greatest total of crops, uses and services."

Pinchot envisioned land and forest management as part of a multi-use policy, where pragmatic and aesthetic results would come from utilizing natural resources to produce the greatest and most reasonable results. Influenced by his own experiences and this progressive-era environmental ideology, Roosevelt envisioned a program that would rejuvenate the glory of America's landscape and revitalize the spirit of the American worker—a multi-use policy similar to Pinchot's. "I propose to create a Civilian Conservation Corps," Roosevelt articulated in a speech in March 1933, "to be used in simple work, not interfering with normal employment, and confining itself to forestry, the prevention of soil erosion, flood control, and similar projects."[9]

Roosevelt may have learned about the federal government's involvement in environmental affairs from his cousin Theodore. During his presidency, in response to the social disorder he saw as a result

of urbanization, industrialization, and immigration, Theodore advocated a "New Nationalism" that reinforced the government's role in systematically improving human, natural, and financial life in America through science and technology. Theodore, and many politicians like him, envisioned that those who had the time and money to invest would lead this social justice movement. It comes as no surprise that Franklin Roosevelt's experiences in Hyde Park in the 1910s and what he saw happening in American society in the 1930s led to New Deal reforms spawned from the ideas of Progressives like Theodore Roosevelt.[10]

As historian Neil Maher argues, the beginnings of the conservation effort that lay at the heart of the CCC came from a group of New England conservationists, scientific professionals, bureaucrats, and wealthy businessmen. These groups saw the consequences of industrialization and urbanization and sought a "gospel of efficiency" that would redirect natural resources to practical and rational purposes.[11] This same ideology existed not only in the CCC but in the Progressive movement of the 1910s and 1920s. There were other connections as well, especially in the Arts and Crafts movement, which developed

CCC boys on VKR bridge, 1936 (National Park Service)

Facing page: The Ledges (photo by Marina Vladova)

in the latter part of the nineteenth century. Oliver Lovell Triggs, a leader in the Arts and Crafts movement, for example, worked closely with Progressives in Chicago at the turn of the twentieth century and believed that "rationalized technological growth did not destroy individual dignity, but enhanced it." There were other intersections as well, but the connection of modernism with the Arts and Crafts movement

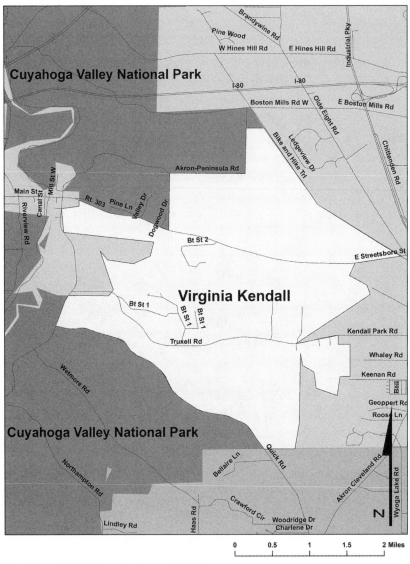

Location of VKR (map by Jason Haley)

and the Progressives outlined a relationship that joined the ideologies of rationalization, industrial growth, and individualism. All of these ideas, of course, lay at the core of the creation and implementation of the Civilian Conservation Corps and the Virginia Kendall Reserve.[12]

The large populations of Cleveland and Akron that sandwiched the Cuyahoga Valley made the idea of a natural recreation area an appealing one. The most likely location for such an area was the Virginia Kendall Reserve, consisting of 530 acres and owned by Cleveland coal baron Hayward Kendall until his death in 1927. Previous to his acquisition of this parcel of land in 1913, the area had been cultivated as dairy pasture by Daniel and Samuel Ritchie, although much of the area remained undeveloped. Kendall bought the land from the brothers for the express purpose of creating a rustic hideaway from his daily position at his father's Cleveland insurance agency. During World War I, he branched out and made his fortune selling coal and continued to use the area as his private escape. When he died of pneumonia, he left the land to his wife Agnes, who had little use for it and turned it over to the state in 1929. In his will, Kendall deemed the land to be called the Virginia Kendall Reserve to honor his mother, perhaps a contributing factor in Agnes's decision to cede the land to the state. The will called for the land to go to the Cleveland Metropolitan Park Board if the state did not take it over, but after some political haggling by Harold Wagner and F. A. Seiberling (founder of Goodyear Tire and Rubber), the Cleveland Park District gave up their claim and, in 1933, the state Assembly gave the Akron Metropolitan Parks Board authority over Virginia Kendall Reserve. Shortly thereafter, Wagner filed an application with the National Park Service for a camp at Virginia Kendall.

Wagner was a graduate of Harvard University's Arnold Arboretum, the most prominent landscape architecture school at the time, and worked for Warren A. Manning, who had worked with Frederick Law and John Charles Olmsted, heads of a prestigious Boston outdoor design firm. Manning focused on using flora as a design element to heighten the experience of the park visitor, and this focus influenced Wagner. The education Wagner received was the most advanced for its era and represented the cutting edge of ecology, as nature had previously been seen only as a barrier to growth or as a commodity. Wagner came to lead the Akron Metropolitan Park District in the

Enrollees arrive at VKR, 1933 (National Park Service)

1920s, and, by 1932, he had transformed the parks, leading the state by planting 255,610 trees. Wagner's CCC application outlined his desire to work with his friend and architect Albert H. Good, who later published the definitive NPS textbook, *Park and Recreation Structures* (1938), on what came to be called "parkitecture." The two sketched out plans for making the Kendall Reserve a recreational destination, with Good designing the structures and Wagner the natural areas, using a 1925 study by the Olmsted brothers created for Wagner's Akron park district. Wagner and Good saw what the Olmsteds had envisioned, namely an area that would provide the visitor with the best natural experience they could create. This became the foundation for the CCC Reserve camp. Recruits began arriving in December of 1933. Identified as CCC Company 576, they began surveying and clearing the land for roads. By the end of summer they had cleared an area for barracks just off of Route 303, south of Route 8.[13]

As the sun faded on the Cuyahoga Valley on December 10, 1933, a train slowly rolled into the center of Peninsula, carrying eight men from CCC Company 576, returning to Ohio after working in California and now joining another two hundred Ohio enrollees. Trucks took the company up a muddy one-lane buggy track to the barracks, and the next day the men braved the harsh Ohio winter and began carving out the Kendall property as their new home. Before they broke in their boots or tested the cots for comfort, the CCC enrollees of Company 576 were in full work mode. They had to be because the Kendall property showed signs of heavy logging and over-farming from the nineteenth century. The land was in dire need of improvement, according to Wagner and the CCC, in order for it to be made useful again. Thus, Company 576 began work immediately by clearing the land of debris, grading for roads, laying water and sewer lines, and building fences. Over seven months of hard work, the boys put up signs and markers, planted trees and shrubs, and converted the old farm houses on Truxell Road into an overnight summer camp. They also built a picnic shelter of local chestnut trees and sandstone, which rested at the northern end of the Ledges. By the end of July 1934, foot trails had been completed, campground facilities erected, and ground for the proposed thirteen-acre lake broken. With schedules set and crews established, Company 576 fell into a routine.[14]

The local community appreciated the result. Mrs. D. E. Davis told a reporter for the *Akron Beacon Journal* in 1942, "I think the CCC boys have . . . made places of beauty at . . . Virginia Kendall Park," echoing many who understood that the CCC had "given us beautiful picnic

CCC arrival at VKR, December, 1933 (National Park Service)

Grading a road for VKR, no date (National Park Service)

grounds . . . and done a service to the whole community by giving
thousands of persons new means of healthful recreation." She concluded by noting that "their work will be appreciated by Akronites
for years to come." James Ulrich, an Akron police officer, agreed,
stating that, "thousands of persons in this area are finding enjoyment
at Virginia Kendall Park . . . their work will be remembered for a
long time." There were financial benefits as well, as Summit County
Relief Director Jacob Zang reported that county families had received
1,185,000 dollars from the enrollees of CCC camps.[15]

The creation and development of the Kendall Reserve fulfilled the
basic requirement set forth by the CCC: the "preservation of natural
features and execution of projects [to] serve the greatest number of
visitors [should be] the guiding objectives of the Civilian Conservation Corps work in Virginia Kendall State Park, near Akron, Ohio."
The boys and men of the CCC knew what type of contribution they
were making to the region. The camp newspaper *The Kendallite,* which
served as the camp's outlet to communicate with the CCC boys, often

contained articles written by the captain and various other administrators outlining the expectations and rules of the camp. It also gave the enrollees an opportunity to express their ideas. Enrollee Joseph Stahl, for example, acknowledged that the "CCC camp has given many young men work and enjoyment, which in turn have done valuable work for the government, not to be estimated only in dollars or progress, but in the sense that it has benefited many people." He and the other recruits felt proud of their contribution to the well-being of the nation and recognized the value their work had in rejuvenating many local communities. Much akin to Winthrop's famous "City on the Hill," the camps saw their work as lighting the way to "make history long to be remembered in the United States." Their work at "Virginia Kendall stands out as a monument of the labor of Company 576," an editorial from the camp newspaper proudly exclaimed in 1937, as "the civilians will enjoy the benefits of this work and the real enjoyment in life is not what you have accumulated in worldly goods but in the pleasure of making someone else happy."[16]

The first major project (after the surveying, clearing of land, and housing) outlined for Company 576 came to be called the Ledges shelter. Initially the camp was under the command of Navy Lieutenant J. R. Tobin, but Wagner found the chain of command required by Tobin difficult to coordinate, and work requests and projects suffered. The cold temperatures in those first few months of 1933–1934 led to complaints by the recruits and irregular work schedules. Wagner, however, felt that Tobin lacked the discipline to get the young men working. In early 1934, Wagner wrote to the second district inspector, who oversaw the district and coordinated with the national office, to complain that while he had "no reason to expect the boys to work under conditions that are not reasonable," he felt the camp commander was making decisions without proper consultation and lacked concern for the schedule. All that needed doing at this early stage was removing felled trees and logs and trying to level the ground so that when the spring thaw came, construction could begin. Tobin's inability to get the work done led to his reassignment in May. His replacement, Army Captain A. W. Belden, would remain with the 576 CCC unit until they were reassigned in late 1938.[17]

Soon after resolving the problem with Tobin, and once the warmer early spring temperatures made work easier, Wagner faced another

The Ledges construction, 1934 (National Park Service)

problem—the CCC region's main office in Indianapolis rejected his and Good's sketches for the Ledges shelter. They had wanted a two-story structure with one side opening onto a covered picnic area, while the main building's large open ground floor would be used for overnight retreats, with restrooms for men and women. They also foresaw a small concessions area and small second-floor living quarters for the caretaker.

When these plans were rejected, Wagner wrote to the fifth region inspector, G. C. Garman, saying he was "very much at a loss to understand why the Regional Office now rejects the design ... when the approval of the construction of a portion of the building was actually made." He then outlined the specific ways in which the shelter was being roughed out and how everyone involved in the project was working toward the original plan's outline.

To change now, he wrote, would set them back considerably and slow work on other projects. After waiting nearly a year, while the unit worked on a variety of other projects in the reserve, the plan finally won approval and work began in July 1936. No sooner had the foundations been laid and wood and other material hewn for the building itself than the region's technical coordinator sent Wagner a new set of plans in September changing again the substance and style of the facility. This time Wagner was irate, writing a bitter letter to the regional officer laced with words like "embarrassed," "delayed," and "disappointed," and challenging the technical coordinator's understanding of the design and landscape architecture in general. "At this time," Wagner wrote, "it is not possible for us to again change our plans and destroy much of the construction as has been completed up to this time, in order to conform to your new ideas . . . [which was caused] solely as a result of the failure of your office to recognize the facts in the case." Wagner concluded by pointing out that the local population had been very supportive of CCC work in the area up to that point and also that a tax levy for the park district and the Kendall Reserve would be on the November ballot and to not move forward would weaken community support.[18]

The Ledges shelter construction, 1934 (National Park Service)

The Ledges overlook in fall (photo by Marina Vladova)

Wagner understood that the bureaucratic interference might have made economic sense, but the regional office's plan did not fit his vision for the reserve. The day after his initial letter he sent an addendum pointing out that "experts" had developed the best design for the area. "I believe that in more than 95% of the cases," he wrote, "in designs like those proposed for the Ledges, the original plan was correct and that those with the proper training understood how to make the area both natural and useful." The reserve had been largely undeveloped and was therefore not useful, and the regional office's proposed revisions, if implemented, would waste the potential benefits of nature that awaited the proper design. As one of the CCC boys recalled, Wagner "knew what he wanted and he knew how to get it too . . . you either did it or you got out." The district office relented.[19]

It must have given Wagner some satisfaction to report in the following year that not only had the Ledges structure been completed, but also that a large natural space for unorganized play called a "playstead," ringed with picnic tables, cooking grills, and benches, had been finished. Wildlife, which Wagner reported had not been seen before 1933, returned; the camp newspaper reported numerous sightings of deer, fox, rabbits, squirrels, and groundhogs. The potential gem of the area, as Wagner wrote in his master plan for the reserve, lay at the southerly end of the plateau, where a lookout or overlook would capture a 180-degree view of the horizon. "From this point," he gushed, "views may be had of equally remote tall buildings in Cleveland and Akron." This overlook would draw visitors to the area to hike trails surrounding it and use restrooms built within viewing distance. While the lookout area was developed, visitors were unable to see either of the city's downtown buildings with an unaided eye.

The area below this scenic outcropping of rocks offered a view of a variety of existing and soon-to-be planted hardwoods rolling down the valley toward the Cuyahoga River, the town of Peninsula, and points beyond. With nearly two million people living "within an hour's drive of it, [the Ledges area] . . . is developed to the point that it is recognized as one of the outstanding operations of its kind in the country." Wagner envisioned that continued usage of the area would pay future benefits, while providing young people with their first taste of nature and uplifting experiences designed to "complete individual responsibility."[20]

CCC construction of Kendall Dam, no date (National Park Service)

Kendall Lake dock (photo by Marina Vladova)

All the while Wagner negotiated getting the Ledges shelter approved and building the playstead, he also worked on a plan to dam up a local creek to create a small recreational lake in the reserve. He hoped that creating a lake might draw people to the area—especially young people—in both the summer and winter. Fed by the Salt Run stream, the area for this thirteen-acre lake had been cleared by the summer of 1934, with a reinforced concrete and earthen dam completed by the fall. "We put 624 cubic yards of hand-mixed concrete," Leonard Tulloch remembers, "taken out and dumped, and dumped, and dumped, and dumped, by wheelbarrow."

The lake filled up quickly and, by the summer of 1935 became a popular swimming area; the bathhouse was completed in 1937. Wagner again ran into problems with the regional office over the bathhouse design, writing in 1936 of how he was "disappointed and disturbed" by the sluggish nature of the office's approval, even after he had incorporated their "further suggestions and changes."

The approval finally came and soon after visitors to the bathhouse were putting their belongings into a wire basket in exchange for a numbered token, while they swam, fished, or lounged on the beach. The CCC worked with the local boards of education to provide city children with their first exposure to the "country parks" by bringing them to the lake. For the opening winter of 1935–36, the CCC also built a toboggan run to augment the ice-skating area. Wagner was excited that the "terrain" had "exceptional possibilities by way of providing for winter sports in a fashion that is not found" anywhere else in the region.[21]

Kendall Lake bathhouse construction, no date (National Park Service)

CCC Company 576, 1934 (National Park Service)

By the end of 1938, Company 576 had completed two shelters, eight latrines, a dam, a bathhouse, seventeen footbridges, a 40,000-gallon well, a 600-foot toboggan run, and 208 tables and benches; graded and developed five acres of campground; moved more than fifteen thousand plants and trees for "effect"; and planted 122 acres of trees all with the desired effect of creating a natural space dedicated to the enjoyment of people.

Although there would be many more projects undertaken throughout the country until the CCC's end in 1942, the transformation of the undeveloped, natural Kendall Reserve into a developed, and by definition, useful piece of nature that was carefully laid out, designed, and constructed to both preserve the beauty of nature and provide pleasure to the people who visited, stands as one of the great successes of the project. Nature, the dominant idea held, was best experienced as a guided experience, and the reserve's camping and dormitory facilities, as well as trails and playsteads, were designed

Kendall Lake bathhouse from the reeds (photo by Marina Vladova)

The Ledges today (photo by Marina Vladova)

to bring in people from area cities for a taste of nature throughout the year. Some would be bused in from their local schools, while others would come by automobile for the day. All of them saw nature as something safe and consumable, like visiting a zoo, or a circus, or, in the modern day, Disneyland. Professionals maintained the area both in terms of overall experience and daily operation. The trails, the vistas, the shelters, and the lake were designed to be enjoyed by nature lovers or simply by those wanting to sample nature.

When this land was first acquired by the Akron Metropolitan Park District, it was undeveloped. Few people came through for a taste of nature. But with planning and vision, and through the labor of CCC recruits, a natural area was made useful. The belief that nature could be made consumable and controlled through organization and planning ties in nicely with the overall modernist design of the CCC, which grew out of the country's rapid industrialization, the Progressive era response, and the Great Depression of the 1930s.[22]

CCC enrollee, VKR, no date (National Park Service)

2

Work Builds Better Men

KENNETH J. BINDAS, LINDSEY CALDERWOOD,
AND MEREDITH SOEDER

Shortly after getting approval for a CCC camp at the Kendall Reserve in the summer of 1933, architect Albert Good pointed out the obvious—the CCC workers would have limited knowledge of and experience with working in nature. He therefore made his initial and revised drawings for the proposed facilities as basic as possible. These drawings proved so valuable to the NPS and CCC that they became the foundational concepts defined, drafted, and pictured in *Park Structures and Facilities* (1938). The basic idea involved using local vegetation to provide cover for outbuildings, blending structures into the natural environment, using local woods for the sidings and shingles, and quarrying local rock for the base. He wrote that he "had made all the truss timbers . . . and rafters squared, rather than round," an easier design feature and one that figured prominently in his designs in *Park Structures and Facilities.*[1]

Wagner also understood that with the CCC he was going to have to rely on largely unskilled, under-educated, and perhaps troublesome, young men. In 1937–38, for example, the national percentage of those enrolled in the Corps who had completed at least eighth grade was about twenty-five percent, with only nine percent competing high school. And they were young. Most recruits were between seventeen to nineteen years of age with little, or no occupational experience.

Roger Sessions, as part of his doctoral research at The Ohio State University, interviewed six hundred Ohio CCC members in 1936–37 to determine their social status and educational training and to argue for increased vocational education in the camps. His study revealed that most enrollees came from families who were unsuccessful in their "struggle for independence and security." Nearly one-third came from traditional working-class backgrounds and another one-third from families who could not list an occupation, were on relief, or worked on the WPA.

Seventy-two percent of these "less fortunate" enrollees came from urban areas and had limited schooling. When 786 Ohio corpsmen were given the Pressey Senior Classification Test (an established mental alertness test used by educators at that time), the median score was thirty-three, which, according to the test's measurement, meant an intelligence level akin to that of a thirteen-and-a-half-year-old in the eighth grade. More than twenty-five percent made scores placing them at twelve years old and in sixth grade, and only a handful scored near their chronological age.

While there were some recruits with what Sessions labeled a "high degree of mental ability," the great plurality came from the lesser strata. This did not mean they were immature or unable to provide for themselves, but they lacked the acuity of many in their age group. Many had quit school before they turned sixteen, and only a few had stayed long enough to graduate. Not that they had left school for employment, as only 173 had jobs previous to their joining the CCC. Of these, they had held jobs in construction, factory work, trucking, or agriculture.[2]

Another study, this time of just Cleveland CCC recruits conducted in 1938 by Helen Walker, associate professor of Family Case Work at Western Reserve University, sheds more specific light on the enrollees likely to be at the Kendall Reserve, since many of those at the reserve were from Cleveland or from similar cities in northeastern Ohio. Given the area's industrial and urban backdrop and that the population of the city grew dramatically during the peak immigration years 1880–1920, it came as no surprise that sixty percent of white enrollees came from families whose head of the household was foreign born, and of the sixty African American enrollees stud-

CCC boys building the Ledges shelter, 1935 (National Park Service)

ied, only one came from a family born in the state. Nearly all came from "lower economic ranges" and from neighborhoods described as "run-down," "congested," and "very close to the factories." African American corpsmen described their dwellings as "crowded, unattractive. Poorly kept, and sparsely . . . furnished." Households were often tense, as divisions between the parents and children arose from the young people's unwillingness to accept their elders' values, be they old world or southern. Many found themselves running with "gangs of boys and young men" and frequenting pool halls, theaters, bars, and city parks. Their parents toiled in working-class occupations, and most came from families of three or more. They generally joined the CCC between the ages of seventeen and twenty, with the median age being eighteen. They fared better than enrollees at the state level, as seventy-two percent had gone beyond ninth grade and fifteen percent had graduated high school. Some had left school because they did not like going or disliked a particular teacher or class, but many others had left because of economic pressure at home.

In other words, they had to work. This is borne out by the fact that thirty-eight percent of the Cleveland enrollees held full-time jobs (albeit temporary, low paying, or unskilled) upon entrance to the CCC, while another eleven percent had part-time employment.

The employment numbers for the African American enrollees conformed to the general numbers for African Americans in the era, as
one-third held no job and the remainder navigated between full- and
part-time work. They were, as one young area recruit said in April,
1933, "Cleveland's not-quite-neglected and not-quite forgotten young
men" getting their first chance at a real job.[3]

Once the young men enrolled in the CCC, not only did they have
to face the task of difficult work under circumstances they were not
used to—outdoors, far from home, and under tight, almost military
control—but since they lived together, they had to deal with the real
issue of getting along. As Roosevelt said, "the Corps is a builder of
the kind of men this Nation needs," and this meant "good moral
character, hard work . . . physical hardihood, active citizenship, and
love of country." They were to be models of the new American. The
commander of the camp reiterated this point in *The Kendallite*, reminding the recruits that "there is a threefold purpose in the development
of the men in the CCC. They must be developed physically, mentally,
and spiritually." Thus the recruits developed physically through
weight gain and muscle development; mentally through work experiences, on-the-job education, and evening classes; and spiritually by
"learning to live and work with other men, and learning to take and
give orders." This agenda worked, according to Leonard Tulloch,
because the CCC boys enjoyed the totality of the experience. They
"wanted to work, and did work."[4]

The Corps leaders trained enrollees to work and the young men
took pride in their accomplishments as laborers, volunteering to make
the camp better even during their hours of free time. *The Kendallite*
honored the workers' dedication, pointing out how they could "boast
of our beautiful lawn, fine walks, writing desks, and recreational
facilities only because a certain group volunteered to do the work."
Since many of them came from working-class backgrounds and from
situations with a strong work ethic, their pride in working for the CCC
shone through and provided them with a sense of social identity.

"We worked almost constantly, everyday, all but Sunday, and we
worked till Saturday noon and late . . . Because we wanted to. Because we wanted to keep going until we got things done." The work
they accomplished served to document the appreciation they felt for

The Ledges shelter from a playstead (photo by Marina Vladova)

their communities, the people, and the trust that the government had provided for them to develop independence and responsibility. The opportunity to work restored the masculinity to men that the Depression had taken from them. Tulloch recalled that the CCC "built a lot of men." The CCC, according to a Cleveland *Plain Dealer* editorial, "yielded human values not measureable in dollars . . . [but] turn[ed] discouraged boys into" productive men contributing to society through their labor.[5]

The boys who came to the CCC needed to be trained not only as workers, but also as men. Historian James Wilson suggests that while the CCC provided employment, money, and potential job skills, the program viewed recruits as "bodies to be molded, shaped, and transformed into ideal American citizens." This meant learning to get along with a variety of ethnic groups and seeing all of them in the same way, at least in terms of being in the same CCC boat. The situation of their enrollment bonded them as a cohort, and this shared identity formed the basis of their unity as a group joined together to work and contribute to American society. In the 1941 Farm Security Administration FSA/CCC publication, *The CCC at Work,* one photo essay ends by noting that the ability to "work and play successfully with other boys their own age is an important part of CCC training" and shows several types of young men planning their weekend together. The rest of the volume is dedicated to showing positive images of CCC men interacting and working together to build the character necessary to be "proud of yourself—and your country."[6]

Building character required discipline and order. Given the backgrounds of many who enrolled in the Corps, this meant teaching them how to follow orders and to understand how following said orders would make them better men. They had to allow themselves to be, in essence, rebuilt. A.W. Belden reminded the recruits at the Kendall Reserve that "Discipline and respect for authority will be impressed upon you. It will not be sufficient to do what you are told—you must do it in the way specified. Follow all orders of those placed in a position to give them."[7]

The focus on training the recruits revolved around a general concern for building masculinity and for how the CCC could project and promote manliness. The loss of work that came with the economic

Creating Kendall Lake, 1936–37 (National Park Service)

Shaping quarried sandstone, VKR, no date (National Park Service)

collapse created what Neil Maher labels a "masculinity crisis" in his study *Nature's New Deal*. He argues that the Corps worked to both protect the nation's manhood and better define masculinity because there was a general perception that the economic crisis had weakened traditional gender roles. The recruits lacked physical conditioning and were underweight and unhealthy, so much so that three-quarters of them would not have passed the basic army weight requirement. Maher notes that "many young men felt both emasculated and infantilized before joining the CCC."

Through hard work and education and training programs, the Corps turned these frail, skinny young boys into strong, tanned, muscular, and healthy men. The strenuous outdoor labor combined with the bountiful food available proved transformative, which, according to Maher, helped them to become "full-fledged workers" in the eyes of the American people and President Roosevelt. And significantly, the emphasis on following orders and a tight schedule also helped build the type of worker necessary to operate factory or farm machinery. As Jeffery Suzik convincingly argues in his article on manliness and the CCC, the "boys were definitely not being encouraged to 'make' technology themselves . . . technology was definitely 'making' them."[8]

"The entire modernist enterprise," writes art historian Christopher

VKR CCC company members, no date (National Park Service)

Wilk, "was permeated by a deep concern for health." This focus manifested itself literally in the design of living spaces and exercise, metaphorically in designs for a better future, and ideologically in the utility of design. In the late nineteenth century, as the discussion over survival of the fittest symbolically pitted men and women against each other, at a time when urbanism and industrial capitalism also encouraged a more sedentary lifestyle, an interest in exercise and fascination with the body as space became paramount. By the beginning of the twentieth century, the body came to be seen as something to manipulate, change, alter, and improve through diet, exercise, and other health therapies.

As the new century progressed, many compared the function and abilities of the human body to a machine, with its efficiency and productivity. By the time of the creation of the CCC, it was widely held that a healthy body was central to the flowering of humanity and was to be derived through a scientific diet, various forms of exercise, and the construction and utilization of living spaces and parks. Increasingly, the image of a tanned, well-defined, and honed body became identified with modernity and opposed to the flaccid, sloppy, and languid body of the wasteful past.[9]

The young boys enrolled in the CCC were quickly transformed,

Kendall bathhouse in winter (photo by Marina Vladova)

being convinced of, or perhaps even converted to, the belief that through environmental planning, hard work, and a healthy scientific diet, anyone could be made into a better, stronger, healthier man. The average corpsman in Ohio gained almost sixteen pounds during his six-month tenure and developed a tanned and muscular body. Ohio recruit Albert Petoski quit school after the ninth grade and after working a variety of jobs fell in with a bad crowd and soon ran afoul of the law. He joined the CCC to escape this lifestyle and remained for two years, leaving with specific skills he could apply in the private sector. When interviewed after his discharge, he said that the Corps had built up his "self-respect," given him a sense of "pride in accomplishment," and "improved his health." He emerged from the CCC a new man, one ready to tackle the hard problems in life and willing

Laying quarried sandstone, no date (National Park Service)

to sacrifice for the betterment of society. Part of being this new man meant becoming a model citizen, projecting the positive ideal that humans can, through the successful completion of simple tasks, done with the proper guidance and the right focus—like preserving the nation's natural resources—make all things better. Petoski, like nearly three million other CCC recruits, became part of the new model army of American citizens dedicated to making society more useful and efficient, while at the same time, transforming themselves, through their work in nature.[10]

"As muscles hardened," Roosevelt told the American people in his radio address honoring the third anniversary of the CCC, the recruits became "accustomed to outdoor work [and] grasped the opportunity to learn by practical training on the job." They were transformed, and their work had forever changed the country for the better. For the young men at the Kendall Reserve, the president's comments held true, as a result of their work, the average enrollee gained nine to ten pounds. Tulloch recalled that the recruits "came in here [the Kendall Reserve] skinny, scrawny, underfed" and within a few months were transformed into men who resembled "weight-lifters." The physical transformation was matched by a change in the way the boys saw each other and the work they were doing. They began to recognize with great pride what they were part of, and they saw in their labors a benefit not only to their generation, but to all those that would follow. Since many of the young men came from troubled backgrounds with little positive reinforcement, they felt proud of their accomplishments and were convinced that through hard work, sacrifice, and planning anything could be accomplished and anyone could be transformed. "I am confident," Robert Fechner wrote in 1938, "that this program has been of great social significance . . . [to] thousands of Ohio enrollees" as it had built up their self-respect and dignity, and brought pride to their families and communities.[11]

The majority of the CCC boys were hard workers, as Tulloch noted: "The best workers I've ever had . . . they hardly said a word all day long, they just worked . . . they really liked to produce, and they did produce." Those who did not work were called "goldbrickers" and supervisors separated them so as not to infect the others with their

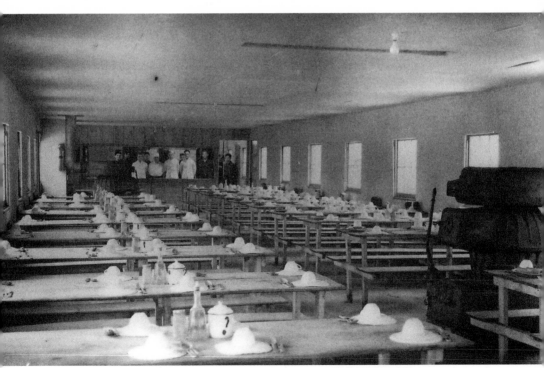

Dining hall and staff, Happy Days barracks, no date (National Park Service)

bad habits. Pulling them away from the group allowed their supervisors to pay extra attention to them, encouraging their conformity to the general program. Peer pressure, however, was the main force for conformity. Tulloch recalled that the Kendall Reserve "had very few goldbrickers [because] the other men wouldn't put up with it, they wouldn't tolerate it [so] they taught them how to work . . . worked beside them and they learned to work." According to the Walker study, there were only about a dozen of these cases in the camp, and after the supervisor separated them and kept them busy with odd jobs throughout the camp, the "policy helped solve the problem of what to do with them." Walker concluded that "at the same time, [removal] kept them from weakening the morale of the other workers." The odd jobs varied from the usual work so that the goldbrickers "did not find it too monotonous, and were apt to complete the job." These boys learned how to labor, and with the guidance of their supervisor, became successful workers.[12]

The leaders of the CCC recognized that the recruits worked best when they could attach a personal interest to their jobs, so supervisors motivated and rewarded hard workers by giving them job preferences. Tulloch remembered his discussion with his supervisor upon receiving a promotion: "He said, 'you deserve something,' and said, 'you've done a real good job'. . . . And I said 'I would like to go into the forest, I'd like to work in the timber if there's that kind of work.' He said, 'Oh, there's that kind of work, that's why we're here.'" The supervisors at the Kendall Reserve understood that the men were most efficient and produced better results when they enjoyed the work they were doing. Walker's study documents the CCC's practice of trying "to give the boys the opportunity for a variety of jobs in line with their interests. . . . If a boy did not perform well at a given assignment or did not appear to be adapted to it, he was nearly always shifted to another assignment." By providing workers with the opportunity to learn skills that interested them, the CCC camps functioned efficiently, helping to prepare a future workforce. The work kept laborers focused and made them feel like they were doing something worthwhile. F. J. O'Leary remembered, "I liked firing the boiler . . . that run the sawmill . . . I liked to keep the steam up . . . and that worked out pretty good. See they take . . . like a quota you'd go to work—I'd go down and get the boiler down—so I'd accumulate a little extra time, and that would be time; there's no extra pay, you take in one week's time, I might get an extra day."[13]

Camp supervisors aimed to expose enrollees to many different types of work, including cooking, office work, road construction, carpentry, nursery work, and quarrying. "By actually experiencing and learning different types of work," the camp newspaper told its readers, "an enrollee may be helped to choose and prepare for his life work." In this way, the CCC worked to funnel these young workers into the private sector by providing them with the necessary work skills and pride. The supervisors regularly reminded the recruits of this larger purpose, using the camp newspaper to underscore that through the CCC they had "an opportunity to be taught the

The Octagon in winter (photo by Marina Vladova)

CCC boys to men, no date (National Park Service)

fundamentals in connection with the job you are doing in the field. The object in giving you this project training is to increase your efficiency so that you may produce more work: be a part of a better and smoother functioning organization; and make each and every one of you more employable." Walker and her group found that nearly three-quarters of the enrollees believed the work they were doing in the CCC would benefit both themselves and their communities.[14]

The sense of duty, purpose, and responsibility enrollees gained helped to hone another important benefit of being in the CCC, namely the opportunity for the boys to grow as men. The experience gained by many of the young men in the CCC encouraged the feeling of self-confidence that came with providing support to their families, changing the landscape of natural communities, making the land more productive, and creating opportunities for the next generation. Many of these young men came of working age during the Depression and felt insecure about their abilities as men because society identified masculinity with earning a living. But because of the economic crisis, these young men found themselves unemployed and socially emasculated. America treasured the virtues of self-reliance and independence, and chronic joblessness placed these boys outside society as respected adults. The CCC provided them with a chance to regain their masculinity and earn a living for themselves and their families. The enrollees were grateful for the opportunity to work and learn, and they felt the joy the results of their labor brought to others. These experiences transformed the enrollees from boys to men: "Most [of] all benefits, [however] are grouped under physical, mental, and spiritual development—which is the primary purpose of the CCC to the young men of the United States."[15]

The CCC altered the American public's view of these young men from potentially dangerous and weak to financially independent, physically developed, and successful men. Their work experiences in the CCC sparked their emotional development and working together made them feel as though they were contributors to society.

Edwin Randall of the *Plain Dealer* wrote that the CCC recruit was able to come "out of the poisonous fog that overhangs idleness" and with hard work, good food, and the rejuvenating spirit of nature was

Army and civilian staff at Happy Days, no date (National Park Service)

"wip[ing] out the bitterness of poverty." The hardships that the men encountered previous to enrollment encouraged them to make the most of their experience in the CCC. In a letter to the editor in 1934, two recruits succinctly outlined the larger value of the project: "It has given [us] a new start in life, a chance to go forward and upward and look the world squarely in the face." Many agreed and saw in the Corps their opportunity to change the path of their lives. In reflecting on his life, Terry Montaquila told his interviewer, "I've never regretted being born in my era, I tell you. It made you appreciate things in later life."[16]

The voices of both President Roosevelt and the army were evident in the expectations outlined to the CCC boys. This rhetoric was an additional tool in shaping the boys into the American men that Roosevelt and the public hoped for. This was evident right from the start, as A. W. Belden, writing in *The Kendallite,* informed enrollees of the camp's goals and expectations: "You must accept the fact that conditions are new, and fit yourself into the picture. . . . Remember,

CCC tents at VKR, no date (National Park Service)

CCC flag raising, Happy Days, no date (National Park Service)

however, that your success here depends on you—stand on your own feet. . . . Remember that you are important, individually, only to the extent that your efforts improve the company as a whole. You can become a very important cog in a well-oiled machine."[17]

The CCC found much of its direction not only from the positive nature of hard work, but the disciplined practices that came through military-style organization. While the size of the United States armed forces was small, and there was lingering anti-war sentiment left over from World War I, the United States military, and particularly the Army, played a dominant role in the administrative and functional makeup of the CCC program. Their involvement was highly controversial until the late 1930s, when they were replaced with CCC men, as many feared that these young men were being taken out into the woods and being trained as soldiers, much akin to the USSR's Young Pioneers or Hitler's Youth Camps. FDR and Fechner sought to ease these fears by reassuring those who feared the military's role that the primary purpose of the Corps was in fact to create jobs. By creating an institution that provided America's youth with the opportunity to work, however, the CCC also had to transform its young enrollees from boys into what America perceived as men. And in 1933, there was no better institution in place to help create a culture conducive to the construction of manhood than the American military.

The CCC camps modeled a military institution primarily through the establishment of daily routines, assignment of commanding officers, use of terminology, and their basic structural setup. The most prominent military characteristic could be seen in the daily operation of the camps themselves. CCC enrollees began each day with the sounding of reveille. Once awake, they were responsible for making their bunks, performing necessary hygiene activities like washing, shaving, and going to the bathroom, eating breakfast, and reporting for "work call" dressed in their military-issue uniforms. This ritual took approximately an hour and forty-five minutes to complete. The recruits would then be sent to their scheduled work detail for the remainder of the day. After eight hours of manual labor, the boys were given the option to participate in on-site educational courses or other leisure activities. Enrollees were not allowed to leave the campsite without permission from their superiors, which usually occurred on the weekends. The call for lights out sounded at ten o'clock in order to ensure that the enrollees received a good night's sleep in preparation for the same routine the following day. The strict regimentation and structure of the daily running of the work camps strongly resembled those implemented on U.S. military bases.

Those put in charge of running the work camps and the terminology they used when describing camp matters were also militaristic. Captains, lieutenants, and sergeants were put in charge of overseeing the day-to-day operation of the camps. They created the schedule for when to eat, sleep, and work, and they also set the rules for maintaining order and discipline. Enrollees were expected to follow the rules set forth by camp commanders and to obey orders without question, as in the military.

If enrollees violated camp rules, the military officers were responsible for implementing monetary or work-detail punishments. Resistance to disciplinary measures or failure to obey orders were considered grounds for possible discharge, either honorable or dishonorable, depending on the infraction. Former CCC enrollee John Derden testified: "The discipline in the Camp was excellent. If you disobeyed an order from anyone in the chain of command . . . you most likely would get a dishonorable discharge."[18] The records indicate that only a handful of recruits were discharged, mostly due to their inability or unwillingness to work. The CCC used other military language to de-

Happy Days barracks, interior, no date (National Park Service)

scribe matters within the camp. Enrollees were called juniors (similar to being called privates), and the groups in which they worked were known as companies. Some enrollees were made to salute their commanding officers, although this was not the norm. That military officers oversaw CCC camps, and an army officer was in charge at the reserve, combined with the military terminology used gave an overwhelmingly militaristic feel to the program.

The final military connection came with the physical structure of the camps, which resembled those found on a military base. The enrollees slept in barracks, showered in communal bathhouses, enjoyed their three squares a day in mess halls, and reported to an infirmary when ill. Military personnel supplied recruits with everything they needed for day-to-day living within the camp. The camps, like military bases, were designed to establish efficient networks of control and work. The CCC enrollees had to adhere to all rules and guidelines and the military personnel demanded obedience.[19]

CCC dress uniforms at VKR, no date (National Park Service)

While it is important to understand how the functional and administrative makeup of the CCC camps reflected those of military institutions, it is also essential to understand why CCC administrators called the military in to run the camps in the first place. First and foremost, they had had experience in dealing with large groups of young men stemming from their involvement in World War I. As each camp consisted of almost two hundred enrollees from different social and ethnic backgrounds, who had spent their lives on the margins of society and were unused to discipline, having the military implement their methods of obedience and control would help the recruits' induction into the CCC, ensuring its smooth and efficient running. This would guarantee that no outbreaks of mass non-cooperation or even violence would take place, tainting the image of this New Deal program.[20]

The CCC administration in Washington also charged the military with running the work camps because they had the physical resources to do so. The U.S. Army consisted of approximately 165,000 men in

CCC flag raising at VKR, no date (National Park Service)

1933. Undersized, it had the surplus command structure available to implement the program efficiently. The military officials successfully executed the tasks allotted them; however, their presence within the camps was not without criticism. There was concern that the government might be using the economic crisis and the corps as a way of enlarging the military and creating a quasi–boot-camp experience to better prepare young men for service. Assistant Secretary of War Harry Woodring heightened this fear when he inadvertently said that the CCC camps were indeed linked to preparedness. While he was admonished by FDR and numerous disclaimers were issued, the specter of government training workers cum soldiers was never completely dispelled.[21]

Unions were also wary of having the military run the camps. The AFL worried, for example, that the CCC was a roundabout way of militarizing labor, building loyalty to the government outside of the union, much the way in which some Europeans countries were using hyper nationalism to weaken worker solidarity. Labor leaders also worried that a military presence would offset the initial objective of the corps: to create jobs. The unions were concerned that military leadership in the camps would create soldiers who might be unwilling to later join their ranks. To offset this perception, and knowing that the support of U.S. labor was vital to the success of the program, Roosevelt appointed AFL Vice President Robert Fechner to head the CCC. FDR's goal was to make sure that leadership at all levels worked to dispel the fear that the corps was a covert attempt at creating a paramilitary organization.[22]

Some political groups also voiced their distrust of the military presence within the corps program. The American Liberty League made correlations between CCC enrollees and Hitler's Brown Shirts, while various Socialist parties cautioned that the camps were a breeding ground for Fascism. It is important to note that the militaristic nature of Hitler's Germany and Mussolini's Italy contributed to public fear of Fascism. It may also explain why Roosevelt made certain that the Department of Labor was responsible for recruiting enrollees and why "CCC officials, from Fechner down . . . tried to minimize the appearance of military trappings" within the program. Anything that could potentially incite mass criticism of the CCC was enhanced by efforts to dispel concerns about a military takeover and to maintain support for the New Deal program. As the decade progressed and the threat of another war loomed, much of this concern dissipated into a tacit understanding that perhaps the CCC and other New Deal programs like the National Youth Administration were necessary national defense mechanisms.[23]

What the CCC did encourage however was camaraderie of the same type that might be found in a military unit. For example, when, in 1935, recruit Red Adams needed to find an adequate spot to drop his truckload of clay, he found a spot near the edge of the lake, but failed to take into account the muddiness of the soil there. As he dropped his load, he found himself sinking into a quagmire up to his knees. William Reed, seeing his coworker's plight, rushed over to help Adams and, after struggling a bit, the two emerged. Although embarrassed and covered in mud, the thought of his fellow CCC enrollee being there for him comforted Red. A month later, on September 27, Jim Kochler discovered a drowning rabbit at the stone quarry. He called over John Morris and within minutes, Kochler lowered Morris into the pit headfirst. After some time, Morris rescued the rabbit and both Morris and Kochler were the heroes of the day.

Stories such as these reaffirm the positive virtues of hard work, togetherness, and responsibility that came with being in the CCC. The enrollees associated these traits with being identified as masculine within their homes and communities. Working together united the men; they saw in their labor the new world they were helping to create. "It's absolutely amazing the work that was accomplished," Tulloch said in 1979, as he pointed in the direction of Kendall Park.[24] The corps was in many ways an institution designed to create men and to prepare them for the labor-intensive work ahead. The army issued mandatory physicals—which the enrollees had to pass in order to continue in the program—and the pseudo–boot-camp atmosphere, with its physical conditioning and abundant food made certain that new men were indeed the byproduct of CCC membership.[25]

These boys grew up in a time plagued by the fear of war, uncertainty, and economic hardship. They were introduced into a new environment and were surrounded by others who, to a large extent, were in the same boat. The army's decision to begin these boys' journeys with group-oriented, health-building procedures suggests that they realized the need for the boys to get along and feel as though they were part of a unit. The importance of camaraderie can be seen in the introduction to the CCC handbook distributed to all new enrollees: "Learning to get along with 199 other men without hurt feelings or broken noses is one thing every enrollee must learn while in camp. CCC camp life is a healthful one. It offers many opportunities for self-improvement, physically, mentally, and vocationally. Boys who "can take it" will get much out of the CCC. They well may be proud to belong to such an organization."[26]

While creating camaraderie within the corps was important, establishing unquestioning obedience was central to the military's goal. Without this command, CCC recruits might not have adjusted so easily to the strict regimentation of camp life. Conditioning in the camps was a way in which to begin the corporeal transformation of the enrollees from boys to men and to construct enrollee obedience and responsibility, the latter being an important characteristic of American manliness. Other factors played key roles in developing a positive attitude, such as the development of healthier physical conditions stemming from three large meals a day, prepared and distributed by army personnel and recruits, and manual labor. They worked forty hours per week in tasks overseen by the Department of Agriculture.

Historian Karin Patel argues that "not only were participants needy, they also belonged to groups that posed a potential threat . . . [the Roosevelt administration and] large segments of the American population feared a growing radicalization . . . in the eyes of many contemporaries, it was especially young males and veterans who were at risk of falling into crime and political extremism—hence, they were dangerous."[27] Providing the CCC with necessary military personnel and structure helped ensure the success of the corps and kept the CCC boys off the streets and out of trouble. The effort to use the CCC to build up a sense of manhood in the nation's young men had ramifications beyond the patriotic or social, as it also made for better workers. The positive effect of having the young men work in nature, combined with a carefully constructed educational program, indoctrinated a new generation of working-class men. The corpsmen learned to adhere to working-class standards of production, take orders, and work as a cohesive unit, all of which served to transform these once unproductive boys into functional producers in a consumer-based society. This can be seen in other

Shaping men, no date (National Park Service)

ways, too. For example, the understanding they developed about the role of nature underscored their understanding of the value of work and its social meaning. Just as factories came to define functionalism through a highly efficient layout and organization, so too did CCC camps like the Kendall Reserve, by turning nature into a finished product under the supervision of skilled staff members. Directed by the technical staff, the boys at the Kendall Reserve sought to tame nature in order to create a natural oasis fit for public use.

The person assigned to oversee the environmental work at the reserve, under Wagner's authority, was Superintendent F. E. Smith. Smith held an advanced degree in landscape architecture from The Ohio State University, and, working with his construction foremen, Luman Cranz and Roland Arnold; quarryman, Irving Humphry; and camp engineer, Archie Ranney, he trained the recruits to become diligent, if not skilled workers. The primary administrators and skilled technicians knew that the CCC boys would lack training. Harold Wagner noted that "we certainly knew that the boys couldn't do a lot of things . . . they had no idea about anything." They were undereducated and unemployed, unable to do highly technical work. So, Smith and the staff broke their projects into smaller, menial tasks, contributing to the larger production goals, just as an assembly line allowed factories to pump out products. By asserting their roles as skilled technicians, the staff at Virginia Kendall equipped the enrollees with some degree of basic specialized training. The enrollees' productiveness was easily measured by the planting of grass seed and trees, shoveling of dirt, and clearing of dead brush. By learning to labor outdoors for eight hours a day, five days a week, the enrollees were in fact being conditioned to the long and tedious work hours they would encounter as industrial workers. Commander Belden, for his part, put their effort into larger perspective, noting the importance of "discipline and respect for authority," and reminding the recruits that each individual effort was only important if it contributed to the production of the whole camp, helping it to operate much like a "well-oiled machine." The camp became a factory, with each enrollee contributing to a small piece of production, as he would working on an assembly line.[28]

It was important for the government and the CCC to accept the responsibility for training the enrollees, as many of them were disillusioned by the lack of employment opportunities and the otherwise hopeless situations in which they found themselves. Wagner saw many of the boys coming into Virginia Kendall as victims of "parental delinquency," leaving the enrollees with few good role models of working-class men. Wagner understood that without some sort of positive intervention they would quickly succumb to criminal and other socially destructive behaviors. Hard work and the discipline of the CCC camps fit the bill.

The whole structure and design of the camp was to turn the boys into competent men and hard workers. Even the scope of classes offered at the Kendall Reserve (see chapter 4) encouraged their place within the industrial workforce. Like the trained technical staff, the educational overseers worked on honing basic skills through introductory academic courses, specifically English and mathematics, so that they would have enough knowledge to get and hold a job. Allowing the boys to earn credits toward a high school diploma emphasized the importance of getting just enough education to qualify for an industrial job, which would provide them with a steady income and help reinvigorate America's industrial production. But perhaps the most important lesson taken away from the educational program was how to take direction and follow orders. By attending class on a regular schedule, two to three nights a week for three months at a time, the enrollees applied the self-discipline encouraged throughout the camp. Moreover, sitting quietly in class and listening to a skilled instructor reinforced their ability to listen to their superiors, as they would have to do as industrial laborers. These efforts evidently paid off, for in 1938 nearly a dozen former enrollees obtained work in areas they trained for while at camp.[29]

Camp life taught the young boys self-reliance, discipline, and responsibility. Following camp rules and being present at all mandatory camp functions, combined with their willingness to commit themselves to the camp's regimentation, helped build their self-confidence. Former enrollee Harry Jenks commented that even though the strict living conditions within the camps sometimes got to him, his decision to stick it out "proved to him that he was 'a man,' and bolstered his self-confidence so that he believed that he would always feel more adequate than ever before in his life." Similarly, enrollee Floyd Bendik lauded his experiences in camp, saying, "most important of all, it taught [me] to accept discipline and authority . . . [and] increased [my] self-respect and self-confidence, and it taught [me] how to get along with people."[30]

View of Kendall Lake from Kendall shelter, 1937 (National Park Service)

3

Creating Nature

KENNETH J. BINDAS, MEREDITH SOEDER,
AND MICHELE CURRAN

The creation and operation of the CCC was multifaceted. The previous chapter explored the interconnection between the positive masculine values of work in a modern society and the desires of local and federal administrators to transform nature and provide hope to the nation's young men. This interconnection exposed the underlying belief that through organization, planning, and reasonable expectations, anything or anyone could be made functional and useful. With the application of scientific reason, there is no waste; everything has a part to play. The CCC prepared young men to work in factories, and it was inseparable from its other goal, namely to make nature more useful, functional, and, to a large extent, consumable. These goals, which FDR identified in his executive order as "for other useful purposes," involved the promotion of the ideals of modernism, which was in part tied to the development of a more modern environmental policy. The president and his advisors—born and educated in an era of rampant industrialism and multiple attempts at reform—saw nature as something untamed, wild, and therefore not very useful. In order to make it useful, either for pleasure or industry, it was necessary to remake nature as modern, controlled, designed, and authentic. In other words, nature, in the eyes of many within the CCC, needed to be made more 'natural' than in its wild state. This was the ecology of the day. The CCC saw its labors as part of the new world that science and reason had defined and the Corps's landscape engineers and National Park Service planners saw the chance to remake, or at least redefine nature with the modern image in mind: a place made safe, useful, and functional. Theirs was not an utopian agenda, but a practical, logical, reasonable reformation of the role and place of nature in the new consciousness taking hold during the Depression era. "Our forests," Roosevelt wrote in 1937, " . . . have been and continue to be a part of the basic pattern woven into our national fabric . . . [and the CCC] is helping to rebuild our youth as well as our forest resources," shaping the future for both.[1]

The intersection of practical need and what Roosevelt saw as "the moral and spiritual value of such work" underscores the role and influence of modernist ideas within his administration and set the tone for the social and cultural reformation that reached its apex during the Depression era. Key to this process was the incorporation of experts such as landscape architects who had graduated from the best colleges and universities, were schooled in the most recent environmental theory, and were dedicated to the planning, design, and oversight of the areas under CCC authority to help transform, according to historian Phoebe Cutler, "what had been largely a creature of chance into a synthesis of orderly design." These experts were instrumental in the CCC's mandate to balance the recreational needs of the people with the desire to preserve or at least maintain the wilderness. They applied this policy throughout the country, hoping to do what the planners at the Kendall Reserve sought to achieve by transforming an undeveloped and abandoned area to one "designed . . . to choreograph visitors' experiences . . . [and encourage] the aesthetic appreciation of landscapes and allow [for] the spiritual communion with nature."[2]

The CCC sought to remake nature in much the same way that industrial designers like Albert Kahn remade industrial production, most famously identified with the Ford Motor Company. The field of landscape architecture was developed in the mid-nineteenth century under the leadership of Frederick Law Olmsted. As with other professions, its members formed an accreditation and oversight organization called the American Society of Landscape Architects in 1899. This new profession blended the mathematics of engineering and drafting with the aesthetic of the gardener, the architect, and the naturalist. As a technical profession, its practitioners applied scientific

Restroom at the Octagon shelter (photo by Marina Vladova)

principles to the design and arrangement of natural spaces, resulting in environments that were "useful, safe, and enjoyable."[3]

Terry Smith, in his examination of industrial design and its social and cultural acceptance during this period, suggests that a natural evolutionary line can be drawn from Ford's River Rouge factory to the "World of Tomorrow" at the 1939 New York World's Fair. Within this nearly four-decade period, the representational and symbolic meaning of modernism "secured increasingly ordered patterns of reading from those consuming them" until it became normal. The CCC applied this idea of modernism to its projects and, in order to better outline its modernist desires, asked Albert Good, who had been appointed to the State Park Division of the National Park Service shortly after his initial work with Wagner for the reserve in 1933, to compile an edition of best practices and designs that should be utilized in reimagining nature. *Park Structures and Facilities* (1935, later republished as *Park and Recreation Structures* in 1938) was divided into three sections, fourteen chapters, and filled with illustrations for nearly every type of building design. Good's compilation outlined how to create "parkitecture" in harmony with the natural surroundings, to blend in with the local flora, and to utilize as much local product in construction as possible. This meant locally mined stone for the footings and vegetation cultivated specifically for the region to augment the built structures (for public use) and yet remain natural. This would give the area a sense of timelessness while allowing the best usage by the largest number of people. The style should, according to Good, "through the use of native materials in proper scale, and through the avoidance of rigid, straight lines and over-sophistication, give the feeling of having been executed by pioneer craftsmen with limited hand tools . . . [to achieve] sympathy with natural surroundings, and with the past."[4]

Wagner and Good used this ideal for the Kendall Reserve. Their plans redirected the viewer's gaze to where they wanted it to fall. They wanted to direct the tourist, the hiker, and all other visitors to the park through a logically designed and reasonably situated natural, modern experience. From the widening of the roads leading to the entrances to the facilities to the arrangement of the parking lots and shelters, Wagner determined the flow of the visitor's natural experience. Under his guidance and with Smith's direction, by 1936, the CCC had laid out nearly five-and-a-half miles of trails throughout the reserve and had planted or moved more than 57,600 trees and shrubs over a seven-acre spread. They also cleared debris and dead growth from another forty-five acres, taking the dead American chestnut trees to a

CCC-built bridge over Salt Run, Kendall Lake, no date (National Park Service)

Windows, the Octagon shelter (photo by Marina Vladova)

local saw mill for use in the construction of the shelters. The lake and beach required six thousand cubic yards of earth to be moved for the earthen dam and enough sand for a thousand-square-foot beach. As visitors came to the reserve and hiked, picnicked, or swam, they did so with the mindset that what they were experiencing was natural and authentic, and unaware that what they were experiencing followed the same basic structural development of the Ford factory designed by Albert Kahn. The CCC's directive to manage nature and make it accessible to the general public fit perfectly with this functional image.[5]

The designers of CCC projects were aware of how their role in the construction of nature fit into the larger goals tied to modernity that permeated other programs of the New Deal. Roosevelt and his various advisors approached the problems caused by the economic collapse with a belief that through reason, logic, and an understanding of the basic natural laws, society could be made to be more responsive to the needs of its people and more efficient in its operation. Items for use, whether tangible, like a school, or intangible, like an experience at the Kendall Reserve, could be created in ways that guaranteed uniformity through the application of modern ideas. The design and layout of the Kendall Reserve ensured that visitors would find the park useful, beautiful, and natural to the point where they would be almost unable to differentiate between what the CCC had created and what had existed beforehand. The CCC and its park designers fully embraced the American style of landscape architecture, which sought to "harmonize with the natural setting" and to create usable, natural areas. To this end, they planted native shrubs like honeysuckle and trees like dogwood, maple, crabapple, and a variety of pines.

Wagner also made sure that all the sandstone used was produced from quarries in the local town of Peninsula, as well as a quarry within the reserve that the CCC developed when it began creating the winding rock stairs that became a landmark for the Ritchie Ledges area. The Happy Days camp structure, the largest of the shelters built in the reserve, is set in the far corner surrounded by trees, almost perfectly matching the design theory of the American school which advocated that built structures should blend into the environment and not de-

VKR Happy Days shelter from Route 303, 1937 (National Park Service)

tract from the naturalness of the area. It features a low-slung roofline that appears as though it has always been there. "Rustic in nature," as National Park historian Jeff Winstel writes, "as the visitor walks toward the building it seems to rise out of the ground, so effective are the building materials and the manipulation of the structure's setting as creating a sense of harmony between the natural and manmade elements of the environment."[6]

The Virginia Kendall Reserve contains several buildings that exemplify the fallacy of the notion that man must retreat to nature in order to escape the modern world. Winstel notes that the reserve's architecture grew out of early twentieth-century ideas of landscape design that "guided the development of the recreational facilities; the buildings read as elements of the landscape rather than the landscape merely framing the buildings." In essence, this era's landscape architects believed that architecture became an element of the landscape and not actually the landscape itself. But where Wagner, Good, and Smith deviated from these ideas and how the designs can be seen as more modern comes from their willingness to dissolve the separation between landscape and architecture. While it is true that the reserve embodies early themes of landscape design, where buildings and other features are intentionally placed within nature to complement it, the designers also employed more modernist ideals, which sought to unify the architecture and nature, eliminating the artifice of separation. The buildings were of nature—made from local stock, surrounded by local flora, and built by local CCC men.[7]

The buildings of the Virginia Kendall Reserve are excellent examples of the modernist parkitecture movement. Take, for example, the Ledges shelter, a visitors' lodge designed by Good. In drawing up the plans, Good wrote to Wagner in March 1934, saying that he would "make the building as simple as possible, leaving off the superfluous and gadgetry." The key for Good and Wagner came in the planning, where a simple yet functional design ensured the shelter could be built. The emphasis for virtually all CCC projects, and in a larger sense all New Deal programs, was on the production process, which predicted the value of the end-product. In the reserve, this meant shelters, playsteads, trails, lakes, and trees. In order to ensure that these end-products would meet the planners' desires, they had to make certain that the planning process accounted for all aspects of

VKR Ledges shelter construction, no date (National Park Service)

the project. For Wagner, this meant having a master plan. In his letter to the inspector for the Branch of Planning and State Cooperation in Ohio, Wagner wrote that the work at the reserve was "intended to serve large groups rather than family picnics," and so the structures and features of the design had to fit this potential usage. Before anything was built, or any trail laid out, Wagner knew exactly how the reserve would be used.[8]

Another building that exemplifies the modernist ideals of the reserve is the Octagon. Winstel notes that its "naturalistic design influences, the original use of the octagon form for shelters can be traced back to [landscape design pioneer Andrew Jackson] Downing. The multiple sides and lack of primary elevation afford wide views and help the structure blend into the surroundings." This stylistic application was developed in the early part of the last century, most famously at Henry Ford's Greenfield Village. Ford wanted to create a village he believed replicated pre-industrial life, a romantic reversion to the simpler, less mechanical times of the nineteenth century. The Octagon shelter also fit this sentiment, as it looks as though it was built by a "pioneer craftsman with limited hand tools." Designed by Good, and replicated with local modification in many CCC park structures throughout the country, the design borrows directly from this strain of modernist vernacular architecture, also sometimes labeled folk architecture.[9]

This architectural style follows the precepts of, as modernist Laszlo Moholy-Nagy wrote, a house being a "practically-constructed biological organism," which "must also contribute to the enhancement of the occupier's energies and the harmony of his activities." Moholy-Nagy's understanding of modernism embraced the natural, and his architectural designs worked to create an organic, natural built environment. The Art Moderne style shunned natural materials in their designs and artifacts, favoring constructed elements like steel, cement, and glass. But, by the 1930s, writes art historian Tim Benton, "many architects tried to capture the essential intimacy and naturalness of vernacular building, while introducing a modern approach to materials and the controlled appreciation of nature." The influence of Finnish designer and architect Alvar Aalto tempered the perceived coldness of Art Moderne styling and created an appreciation for the "positive influences" of nature and natural materials. The work of Frank Lloyd Wright during this period is an example of this "organic architecture," which used design models built upon a relationship with organic materials and modernist thought. The combination of natural materials, simple and useful designs, and the incorporation of

Octagon shelter roof, no date (National Park Service)

The Octagon shelter (photo by Marina Vladova)

local materials played a central role in this new style and are evident in Good's designs for the CCC in the buildings it erected at Virginia Kendall Reserve.

Because the CCC constructed the reserve buildings out of local dead and decaying American chestnut trees, they unconsciously adopted the naturalistic and localized style endorsed by Moholy-Nagy's ideal of "practically constructed biological organism." So, in addition to meeting its of improving the natural landscape and making the reserve useful for the public, the CCC also recycled natural resources in the area to build these pioneer-inspired, yet modern, buildings.[10]

The structures built by the CCC in the Virginia Kendall Reserve aided the larger program goal of designing a useful natural experience and provided places that, as Moholy-Nagy described regarding structures in general, contributed to the "enhancement of the occupier's energies and the harmony of his activities." One excellent example of how the CCC worked to manipulate nature to heighten the visitor's experience can be seen in the construction of an overlook or vista at the Ledges area. Wagner wanted to utilize "the southerly end of the plateau" to create an overlook so that hikers and visitors might look out and see the "tall buildings in Cleveland and Akron." He wrote this in the master plan, indicating his desire to control the way nature was to be viewed and experienced at the Ledges area. Wagner might have taken his cue from Henry Vincent Hubbard's 1929 study on landscape design, in which he noted that "framing a vista eliminated visual intrusion of undesirable objects in addition to defining the limits of the composition. . . . These features combined with modest scale trees or shrubs further blend the building and its setting together." This is exactly what Wagner sought to create with his overlook. By having no obstructions blocking the view of nature, he hoped to encourage a spiritual connection to the area, and to emphasize its pure and simple qualities. To create this desired result, the CCC reformed the nature in, around, and below the vista to ensure that the experience would result in awe and wonder. The application of the ideals of modernism to providing places of spiritual solace in nature served as an unintended result of the CCC's work in the reserve.[11]

It fell to the CCC in the reserve to provide a means for the public to experience the spiritual and liberating aspects of nature. For instance, Smith made sure that when hikers came to the reserve, they would experience nature by following trails that skirted around the Ledges and flowed from one area to the next. Wagner and Smith designed these trails intentionally, just as they did the "play steads" or open meadows. As Wagner described: "The upper play stead is distinctly a family picnic area. . . . The open area provides for space for unorganized play, the table, benches and ovens being disposed about the fringes of the wooded land which skirt this area. Water supply, sanitary facilities, parking areas, a year around shelter have been developed by the CCC for this area." These playsteads were not mixed into the wooded area but were placed on the "fringes." By providing a water supply facility, parking, and shelter, Wagner and Smith ensured that the public did not have to revert back to the primitive days lacking in modern comforts to enjoy recreation in nature. Furthermore, the design encouraged visitors to follow the path laid out by the CCC in order to experience the joy of nature. Nature could be shaped by the will of man just as a machine in a factory could.[12]

The very language used in official documents and correspondence at the Virginia Kendall Reserve illustrates how the CCC embraced, though not necessarily consciously, modernism. In his 1935–36 CCC

Kendall Lake construction, 1936 (National Park Service)

report about the Virginia Kendall Reserve, Smith wrote about how each project was designed "to serve," "to confine," and "to care for" each visitor to the area. He and Wagner designed each project to serve a very specific end result: preserving the "natural features [of the area]" in the hopes that the "projects that will serve the greatest number of park patrons and to take them to those places of most interest."

The appropriation of modernist language in their official documents reveals Wagner and his design team's commitment to transforming the reserve through rational planning, simple utilitarian structures, and efficient organization.[13] This understanding of and complicity with modernist ideology is also reflected in Wagner's letters to various regional and state agencies. In a 1938 letter to the regional officer of the Branch of Planning and State Cooperation, Wagner discussed the completion of shelters on the reserve, writing that "you will agree that from the standpoint of utility and appearance, the structure as designed will serve the purpose which is demanded," and further, it "has been in constant use throughout the past summer and not only has given excellent service, but is also the subject of a great deal of favorable comment on the part of lay people and architects alike." Wagner made a point of outlining the shelter's utility, as well as its general approval by the local population. The CCC never deviated from its core mission of salvaging the environment, providing employment, and creating modern, natural, and useful recreation spaces for the American public.[14]

These goals applied to the reserve, as Smith reported to the regional office in 1936, commending his people at all levels for their adherence to sound practice, organization, and planning—all aspects of the modernism that resulted from industrialization. Smith wanted the CCC to develop "adequate picnic grounds and the ample provision for the parking of automobiles." He also reported that it was important to maintain the already established "foot paths [which] have tapped large areas hitherto inaccessible and consequently have increased the number of devotees of these outdoor activities." Even the War Department, which oversaw the daily operation of the camp and its recruits, commented on the modernist features of the reserve.

In their 1935 report, they pointed out that their success was due mainly to the "sound organization" of the camp, as each branch

Door, the Octagon shelter (photo by Marina Vladova)

Construction of restrooms, VKR, no date (National Park Service)

worked much like the "well-oiled machine" Commander Belden had sought to create with the CCC boys. The Department of the Interior's report on CCC work in 1935 agreed, outlining how "specific work projects which have been completed will aid field officers of the National Park Service in an effective manner to conserve and preserve natural features." Each of these reports used modernist language in documenting the planning and functional use of enrollees and equipment and served as a testament to the CCC's goals of redefining and mastering nature. Other governmental departments and agencies under the CCC umbrella reflected the "soundness" and organization that Smith, the War Department, and the Department of the Interior reported in their official reports. The reserve was not unique in this as these ideals were part of the larger function of the CCC throughout the United States.[15]

Modernism is a term often used to describe the industrialization and modernization of American factories and businesses in the 1920s, while the discussion of nature during this time often focused on a desire to revert to pre-modern times, suggesting a separation between nature and industry. But in the 1930s, and under agencies like the CCC, there was a concerted effort to erase this division and unify the ideals of industry—reasonable planning, efficiency, utility, and safety—with the natural world. The CCC in the Virginia

Kendall Reserve exemplified how the rationale that drove modern industrialism could also be applied to nature. Good's architectural designs, Wagner and Smith's outline and design of the park's natural recreational facilities, and the appropriation of modernist language in their official reports detail the effort toward unification of the natural and the machine. Modernism in nature signaled a return to the aesthetic beauty of the world around us; but the ability to experience this beauty came through the application of machine modernism and its themes of efficiency, practicality, and pragmatism. Within the Virginia Kendall Reserve, the public experienced what life was like before the rise of a modern industrial society but did so within a controlled and supervised atmosphere that came about only as a result of modernization.

The CCC's experiences at the Kendall Reserve underscore the administrators' commitment to the idea that nature could be made more useful not just through landscape architecture, but by recognizing that any reconstruction of nature begins with man. Through planning, reason, and a willingness to work together, any problem could be solved and every person saved if only they had faith. Helen Walker's study of those CCC boys from Cleveland concluded that what most of those

Restroom today (photo by Marina Vladova)

interviewed expressed when discussing the CCC was their acquisition of "intangible and broad" values concerning personal development—they felt that they had been transformed. They recognized the value of their work to society and themselves and felt an obligation to tell others about the positive virtues of the Corps. "To me," said one enrollee, "the Civilian Conservation Corps is the beginning of a new era in America," and he was proud to be a part of it.[16]

This pride came from their understanding of the impact they had on the conservation and creation of natural resources. Leonard Tulloch pointed with pride to all the trees in and around the Kendall Reserve and told his interviewer that they "planted all the trees you see there . . . hundreds of thousands of trees." Many of the corpsmen expressed gratification mixed with humility in discussing their work in nature. The CCC actively constructed a natural setting designed to utilize time and space and to create a "parkitecture" that would be useful and efficient, spacious and controlled—modern. The enrollees saw their work as "speedier and more efficient [than] Mother Nature" and were in awe at their own physical and intellectual transformation. They witnessed firsthand the power of planning, organization, hard work, and the development of an ethic that valued working with others. In his final report in January 1944 to Interior Secretary Harold

Kendall Dam and Lake, 1938 (National Park Service)

Inside Kendall Lake bathhouse (photo by Marina Vladova)

Ickes, Conrad Wirth made direct connections to the transformative nature of the CCC—on the boys, nature, and the larger society: "It brought to the minds of the people of this country the need and value of a sound, active conservation program . . . the nation cannot afford to have its resources neglected or wasted . . . this can be done only by careful planning and hard work." The CCC succeeded not only in constructing nature but also in creating millions of eager, proud, and productive American workers.[17]

Kitchen crew, VKR, 1935 (National Park Service)

4

Leisure Is Learning

KENNETH J. BINDAS, STEPHANIE VINCENT,
MICHELE CURRAN, COLLEEN BENOIT,
AND ANDREA HAUSER

Local recruit Al Sommer, recalling his time at the Kendall Reserve, said many of the young men he met in the CCC "could neither read nor write." Literacy and other forms of basic educational skills also played a central role in the operation of the camp. As Sommer noted, "they taught 'em to read and write." In an effort to build self-confidence, pride, and self-sufficiency in the nation's young men, the focus on literacy was part of a larger effort by the CCC to improve the recruits' learning skills in a variety of areas, from semi-skilled trades to sports.[1]

While the primary focus of the CCC concerned making the young men into useful citizens and workers, combined with reclaiming the nation's environment, regional directors and individual camp commanders felt the need to spend significant amounts of time and energy on educational and recreational activities. Fechner and other national leaders were convinced that teaching the CCC recruit certain basic skills, in addition to providing them with competitive athletic activities, would greatly benefit American society. At the local level, the CCC at the reserve wanted the general public to see the camps' benefit as a training ground for recruits, not as a place harboring potential criminals or wild boys who might terrorize the local communities. Townspeople generally welcomed the idea of the CCC being at the reserve, as it brought money into the local economy. The recruits were allowed to go into town on weekends, although there were occasional complaints that the young men drank too much and were aggressive with local women. Wagner wrote to the inspector for the second district, G. C. Harmon, in the spring of 1934 about reports of CCC boys "running up and down the streets and dark alleys at all hours" and suggested that the camp enforce greater discipline and training.[2]

That there was a need for some sort of reeducation was not news to those concerned with the needs of the nation's youth. There was special concern about the benefits and uses of leisure time in the 1930s, as many believed that with the continued introduction of time-saving devices in the home and factory the American people would have much more time to spend in leisure activities. As far back as the 1880s, when Americans began discussing the necessity of recreation and play to create "better" members of society, many suggested that government should take greater responsibility for creating rec-reational programs or park-like facilities to benefit the public. This movement began in earnest in Boston in 1885 and quickly spread to other cities in what came to be known as the "Play Movement."

These first parks were created as "sand gardens" for small children to play in and to assist in their social development. Funded through local philanthropists, these play areas, which were little more than sandboxes, were located in crowded, urban areas. The rationale for the creation of the Boston sand garden, according to the first chronicler of the movement, Clarence Rainwater, was "both for the sake of the children and for the convenience and comfort of the community at large. . . . The children are thereby given resorts where they are safely engaged in their sports without danger to themselves or annoyance to others." Play areas were therefore considered not only a place for the entertainment of young children, but also a place to keep them out of the way of adults.[3]

Within ten years, other urban cities across the United States (like Chicago, New York, and Philadelphia) recognized the benefits of having designated play areas and created their own, based on the Boston model. What started as "sand gardens" evolved into model playgrounds with equipment such as parallel bars, rings, and ladders.

Growing numbers of children began patronizing these urban parks after school and on the weekends, with or without their mothers. They were often organized into playgroups by age and games were supervised by adults employed by the founders of the playgrounds. Sometimes one of the mothers would be in charge, but more often than not, the parks were organized and overseen by experts.

As the number of people using the playgrounds increased, the public came to consider them an essential feature of urban areas. Increasingly, local governments created specific departments focused solely on recreation. As they were a public service, they began to be funded by taxes rather than philanthropists so that money could be spent on the creation and expansion of local play areas. Over time, these departments advocated for recreation for adults as well. Eventually, they coupled their responsibility for the creation and maintenance of playgrounds for children with the building and administration of adult recreational centers.

Urban recreational centers across the United States increased from 201 to 757 between 1910 and 1917. While they were found in only 31 cities in 1910, that number had grown to 113 seven years later. The objectives of these centers centered on the participation of individuals who created their own recreation rather than passively watching others for amusement. Engaging in music, theater productions, local dances, festivals, and pageants helped citizens participate in entertainment, rather than solely observe it. Thus, as early as the teens, there was a social awareness of "bad" versus "good" uses of leisure time. Not surprisingly, the debate over good versus bad recreation came to a head in the 1920s. With movies, radio, saloons, gambling, jazz music, and dance clubs, the public had a wide range of choices to select from when deciding how to spend their leisure time. There was a concern among some who felt that a strong democracy depended upon active participants in society rather than those willing to spend their time and money to be amused. The country needed to focus on developing and creating more recreational programs to benefit society. The tension between these forces tightened during the Depression years, as unemployment skyrocketed and people found themselves with more time for leisure and less money to spend. The Roosevelt administration tried to ease this anxiety by creating several

CCC group photo, VKR, no date (National Park Service)

programs designed to help guide Americans in leisure time activities to promote active civic involvement, while paying workers so that they might stimulate the other, less active, forms of leisure.[4]

The New Deal's focus on getting Americans back to work went hand in hand with finding ways to direct and structure recreational activities. These programs would encourage more proactive citizens and curb the widespread fear that society was deteriorating. FDR and his administration recognized that while the federal government had a responsibility to shape recreation programs in order to strengthen their democracy (especially with the rise of fascism and totalitarianism in Europe), they had to allow local governments to operate and administer the local recreational centers.

As historian Susan Currell wrote, "The key to recovery was deeply interwoven with the way Americans used their newfound leisure: although leisure was the problem, it was also to become the solution." Essentially, FDR's administration was afraid, as were many others, that if Americans had more spare time than ever, and they lacked the proper guidance on the "right" ways to enjoy it, such as by learning a trade, working for their high school diploma, or participating in locally run programs and activities, society could deteriorate. This type of recreation would benefit themselves and, more importantly, society. This was the task for the CCC.[5]

That any organization could take fifty to one hundred young men from difficult backgrounds and sequester them away for periods at a time in an all-male environment and not have problems associated with their wildness and penchant for trouble is hard to imagine. Besides the restoration and conservation of nature that were central to the CCC's agenda, another achievement was its ability to provide the country's young men with an opportunity, as the *Plain Dealer*'s Edwin Randall noted in 1933, to march "into the fresh air of the nation's forest camps . . . [rather than loiter] penniless on a dirty Cleveland street corner." Observers understood the dangers confronting the nation's youth and saw in the CCC an opportunity to rescue young boys "from unhealthy idleness" and provide them with "healthy, gainful occupation[s]."[6]

One of the central goals of the CCC's recreational and educational activities was to teach the recruits to channel their energies away from behavior that normally might bring negative attention to the camp. This meant, first and foremost, dealing with their sexual desires. They were young men, getting stronger and healthier through their labor and government food, who had pocket money for perhaps the first time in their lives, and who were feeling frustrated at least and horny at best. Love and sex were among the more frequent concerns that could lead to trouble for the recruits. In a letter to the advice editor of *The Kendallite*, one young man asked why he was unable to maintain a relationship with a girl after the first date. He was shy and the girls rebuked him because he couldn't "make love to them the right way." Whether he meant sexual intercourse or just making the girl understand his ardor, his letter reveals the confusion that beset many of the young enrollees. And, almost typically, the "Voice of Experience" advised him to make sure the lights were turned low and, for more specific advice, ask "Pete, [as] he makes all 16 year old girls' heart skip a beat."[7]

The first instruction given to all recruits involved personal hygiene, with a particular focus on the prevention of pregnancy and venereal disease. Officers tried to dissuade the recruits from engaging in sexual relations with the local girls by instructing them on the "gravity of venereal disease" for their mental and physical health. To reinforce the seriousness of the disease and its association with sex, the chaplain spoke next reminding the young men to pay "attention to the moral aspects of the circumstances leading to infection." This was a real concern for among Ohio recruits, other than common respiratory issues and flu, venereal disease was the most reported disease in the forty-one camps during 1936, with 120 reported cases. This meant that 18.09 percent of men in the CCC in Ohio in 1936 were diagnosed with a sexually transmitted disease, a slight decrease from the year before. The problem was exacerbated by the fact that many towns still had houses of prostitution, which, according to one evaluator, "did a good business on liberty nights." But for those who refused to follow the advice of the medical staff and Commander, "prophylactic stations" were scattered throughout the camp with the edict that "all men who have had illicit sexual intercourse" must report to the station for "such cleansing and prophylaxis as may be prescribed."[8]

The CCC camps also had the difficult task of trying to rein in some recruits who had come from backgrounds with few or no limitations imposed upon them. They were not used to nor did they like taking orders. But work and life both outside and inside the camps was dangerous and the CCC administrators needed to make the recruits cognizant of the need to follow orders for their own safety. *The Kendallite* reported, for example, that enrollee Patsy Carline had been killed after the car he was riding back to camp in after a Saturday night in Akron collided with a bus, sending him hurtling into a telephone pole. He died "almost instantly." Enrollee Carl Korosech died after diving into Virginia Kendall Lake—the water where he dove was only two feet deep, and he suffered a fractured skull. Thus, the free-spirited lifestyle of enrollees could prove fatal.[9]

The key to preventing these accidents and discouraging inappropriate behavior was education and exercise. The camps counselors had to teach the recruits. The *Manual for Instructors in the Civilians Conservation Corps Camps* made plain their pedagogy—practicing something until it became a "habit." The *Manual*'s authors compared the mind to a "switchboard" that needed to be trained through rep-

Gathering wormy chestnut logs, 1934 (National Park Service)

etition to act correctly. The role of the teacher was to control, direct, and manage the thinking of students in order to make them more willing to accept the lesson.

Many in the Corps, the *Manual* reads, "have developed bad habits" and needed redirection toward better ones. Education played a key role in helping the recruits accept authority and the advice of those in positions to give orders. The Education Program, which designed literacy courses and vocational training, wanted to develop in the recruits an "understanding of the prevailing social and economic conditions to the end that each man will cooperate intelligently in improving these conditions." They taught academic subjects but focused mainly on vocational skills like auto mechanics, typing, forestry, and diesel engineering. The listing for educational opportunities at the reserve appeared in *The Kendallite* under the banner "Kendall Trained Men Succeed," with courses ranging from beekeeping and auto mechanics to boxing and wrestling. In fact, physical activities played a prominent role in education policy, particularly on weekends when recruits had extra free time and energy. Company commanders made sure that there was plenty of athletic equipment available for team sports like baseball, basketball, football, and volleyball, along with individual contests like boxing and horseshoes. Interestingly, tennis, croquet, and gymnastics were neglected, most likely because they catered to a different class than those in the Ohio camps. Yet, some Ohio camp commanders reported that at least one-third did not want to participate in physical exercise on their days off.

Of course there were other events and activities that rounded out the enrollee's time off and kept him nominally out of trouble. The intent was noble—to make them better men and make for a better society. Upon their discharge most reported that they had learned to read more, take better care of their health, feel more confident, and get along with others. The education program, really a training program, was given much credit for these successes. The CCC's incorporation of the recreation and play movement ideals helped directly educate the public—in this case young men—about how to spend their leisure time in ways that helped them grow into productive individuals.[10]

One key source for information about the educational offerings was *The Kendallite*. According to Commander Belden, the camp paper was designed not just to "please you with jokes, cartoons, and scandal," but also to provide useful news and information. The paper worked to educate the enrollees and the first lesson was to follow the rules. *Kendallite* reporter John Hines told readers that a camp without rules was foolish, for they "are for our protection, even if they may seem severe, and unnecessary. So the next time some camp rule gripes us, let us remember that it is for our protection and we must act accordingly, and *PLAY THE GAME*." But over time and as the need for reinforcement lessened, the paper published more human-interest types of articles. One popular feature was an advice column, "Letters to the Voice of In-experience." The columns drew lots of interest and indicate that the enrollees wanted more than just educational information. *The Kendallite*'s staff struggled to find a balance between the "strict journalistic standards" under which they wrote the paper, the external administrative desires, and the collective camp readership. This dilemma echoed the challenge of many print publishers in the larger society of the 1930s.[11] As *Kendallite* editor Joseph Stahl wrote in 1936: "Those who remember the first issue of the paper will say that a great deal of improvement has been made during the past year. . . . Besides news stories, which are written concisely and to the point—instead of rambling, several future articles have added to the paper. These features are 'Who's Who in Co. 576,' 'Work Project,' 'Health Bureau,' 'Voice of In-experience,' 'Nature in the Raw,' and 'Book Reviews' of books to be found in the camp library."[12]

Education, however, was the keystone. By late 1934, the CCC's central administration, under Robert Fechner, with the cooperation of state departments of education, outlined several basic goals for the educational programs:

1. To develop in each man his powers of self-expression, self-entertainment, and self-culture.
2. To develop pride and satisfaction in cooperative endeavor.
3. To develop as far as practicable, an understanding of the prevailing social and economic conditions to the end that each man may cooperate intelligently in improving these conditions.
4. To preserve and strengthen good habits of health and mental development.
5. By such vocational training as is feasible but particularly by vocational counseling and adjustment activities, to assist each man better to meet his employment problems when he leaves camp.
6. To develop an appreciation of nature and of country of life.

The CCC's educational program hoped to train young men to "cooperate intelligently [to] improve" themselves and, by extension, the country. By teaching basic skills and working to help them learn to cooperate, the program intended to prepare enrollees to take their place in the industrial labor system.[13]

Virginia Kendall's educational program, organized by Charles Ufford in 1934, set the tone for educational advisors to follow. He built a strong foundation with several classes and the establishment of *The Kendallite*. Lewis Keck, who replaced Ufford in 1935, came to the Kendall Reserve with an extensive background in education, with a master's degree and five years of high school teaching experience. Keck taught traditional classes focusing on literacy and fulfilling the requirements for a high school diploma, and he added photography and other handicrafts. He collaborated with a librarian at the Akron Library, Virginia Well Collin, to organize the camp's first library, which quickly became a popular feature. Keck later recalled that "our boys were always getting out books" and bragged that "they only lost one." Keck also invited teachers from the Peninsula and Akron area for classes in dancing, cooking, typing, and music. However, the most popular courses among the Kendall Reserve enrollees were English, higher mathematics, and language, as the enrollees understood what was needed to help them find a job. Furthermore, the educational system allowed boys without high school diplomas to earn credit toward their degrees, fifteen of whom did so while at camp.[14]

While the CCC boys began to see their physical transformation first, the education and recreation programs reinforced their new images as productive men. With few options available in the private sector, the boys used the CCC experience, as one Cleveland *Plain Dealer* editorial opined, to gain the "maturity and experience" necessary to prepare to take their place in industry. Enrollees gained confidence through their newly acquired knowledge, as they learned more about their jobs and the world around them, and were able to complete their tasks more efficiently with an understanding of the benefit the country would see through their labor. *The Kendallite* helped remind them that the "CCC enrollee develops mentally through his work, as well as through the educational department." The combination of work and education tuned the minds and bodies of the workers—they were becoming stronger and smarter. The men learned to respect their supervisors because the knowledge that they shared made the men more productive and enabled the enrollees to do the job. F. J. O'Leary liked the system, saying, "they would supervise it; and I liked that . . . I'd go with that." The system also taught them leadership skills and aroused their desire to learn so that they could become capable leaders themselves. Supervisors reminded them, through the camp paper, that "you are important, individually, only to the extent that your efforts improve the company as a whole." Knowing that their labor was essential to the success of the CCC gave them confidence to work toward self-improvement. The positive attitude for learning ran high and attendance in evening courses had reached eighty-seven percent by 1936.[15]

Given the mandated forty-hour workweek and the boys' hard physical labor, administrators wanted to make sure that the enrollees used their leisure time positively, not simply because they needed a break from the toil, but because the CCC saw varied recreation as a means of self-improvement. The National Recreation Association, organized in the early stages of the play movement, saw leisure time as "a remarkable opportunity for human advancement" that affected society as a whole. The Corps leadership understood this and made sure that enrollees had ample time for recreation. In a typical week (unless inclement weather caused work to have to be made up), enrollees had up to three and a half hours on weekday evenings and at least ten hours each weekend day to spend on leisure activities. They usually spent this time in one of three ways: athletics, cultural or educational pursuits, or activities outside the camp in nearby towns. The educational opportunities introduced the recruits to a variety of activities that could help maximize their personal growth and keep them from wasting their time in "bad," passive leisure activities.[16]

Athletics was one of the most popular recreation activities. Many CCC camps had adjacent sports fields for football, baseball, or basketball for the men to play either casual "pick-up" games or organized team competitions in their spare evening hours or on weekends. Sometimes they played against other local teams. The Kendall Reserve had both baseball and basketball teams and played either for the town of Peninsula in baseball and softball tournaments or as a Corps team against other camps in the area, including teams from Youngstown and Cleveland. In softball, the Kendall Reserve faired pretty well, finishing 5–3 in the 1936 season despite the 1–7 record for the hardball team. Company 576 also had a basketball team, which received an invitation in 1936 to join the Class A league in Akron as the Wallhaven Taverns, taking over from the sponsor's previous team. This team played against other small, privately sponsored teams at Central High School in downtown Akron. The focus on team athletics worked to promote the discipline and camaraderie needed to work together in the forests. It also allowed enrollees to build a sense of sportsmanship and cooperation as they learned to work together with their campmates in order to achieve success. Sports such as baseball and basketball promoted movement, excitement, and the release of energy built up over the long workday. It also provided an important release for their sexual desires.[17]

In addition to organized team sports, the men at Virginia Kendall enjoyed more individualized athletic activities. The most popular by far was boxing, practiced both for fun among enrollees and taught formally by an educational advisor on Tuesday and Thursday evenings. According to enrollee Sam Bereznak, part of boxing's popularity was inspired by the arrival of Russ Heiss, an ex–state boxing champion and enrollee, who served as a leader of sorts among his campmates. Swimming was also popular wherever they could find a spot for it in the area surrounding the Cuyahoga Valley, but mostly at Lake Kendall, the lake they built in 1936.[18]

For those who preferred to stay indoors for sport, or for days when foul weather kept the boys inside, CCC camps typically had a recreational room, under the supervision of the educational advisor, stocked with a full array of equipment such as ping-pong and pool tables, cards, checkerboards, a radio, and a small library. At Virginia Kendall, ping-pong and pool were the most popular, so favored, in fact, that a second pool table was added in the summer of 1936 and the existing table refurbished due to excessive use. So important were these activities that large-scale renovations were made to the recreational hall in 1935 and 1936. Not only was new equipment (such as the second pool table) added and existing equipment repaired, but the camp's enrollees also expanded the hall structure to include a reading/writing facility with a magazine rack and benches. They also replaced the ceiling and made it higher for better ventilation. Finally, they added new lighting fixtures and furniture to complete the new space. These improvements document the significance of directed recreation by the CCC as an effort to channel the energies of the young men into positive and "clean" manners.[19]

The Kendall Reserve augmented the recreational opportunities with other, more cultural, offerings. Musical performances often took place featuring singing, instrumentals, and recitation. The recreation room featured a piano, and the men would sing along to its accompaniment, occasionally aided by the few enrollees who had brought their guitars. Occasionally, the men at the camp would put on full shows to entertain each other.

CCC member James Sanderson entertained his bunkmates in barracks #3 in July 1935 with such a spectacular show that the camp newspaper gave it a rave review. The article described how Sanderson's theme for the evening was a taste of India, as he danced in a full "Hindu" costume (baggy pants and a turban made out of a towel and

VKR playtime for talented musicians, no date (National Park Service)

bar of soap) and sang and yodeled to the accompaniment of a guitar and mouth organ provided by his friends. When the enrollees were not entertaining themselves, other New Deal agencies were invited to the camp sometimes to perform for the enrollees. In August 1936, for example, an African American WPA Federal Music Project orchestra visited the Virginia Kendall camp and provided a concert for the enrollees, followed by requests and an old-fashioned minstrel show. These entertaining diversions proved to be, as *The Kendallite* wrote, "unforgettable experiences" for Corps members.[20]

Many men took advantage of any activity that might expand their skills and learning. Photography was a particularly popular class and became a hobby for many in the Kendall camp. Members shot various aspects of the Cuyahoga Valley and the park they were beautifying. The camp classes took place two evenings a week, and the enrollees were taught to use the camp's darkroom and developing lab. The interest in photography generated in the camps spilled over to their later lives, as many enrollees reported that they continued the hobby after completing their time in the Corps. Others made use of the camp's library. Many CCC camps had permanent or mobile libraries, with books usually falling into nine general categories: adventure/mystery, fiction, westerns, history, science fiction, athletics, religion, and periodicals. Virginia Kendall had a permanent library in the recreation area, which began as a small cache of books on loan from the Akron public library. Due to enrollee interest, the camp developed its own permanent collection through funding from the educational advisors and private donations. In 1936, the Virginia Kendall library received an additional forty-six books from Parker Lowell and A. L. Walker, making it, according to the camp newspaper, "one of the finest and most complete libraries to be found in the Corps area." While the enrollees found the camp library more than acceptable, some criticized the lack of classics or political tracts to properly stimulate the intellects of the men at the camp. Regardless, enrollees utilized the library resources, and many who had entered the camp without a high school diploma used the facility to improve their reading skills and earn their degree. As former camp member F. J. O'Leary said, the CCC was the "best thing that [the government had] ever done. . . . The opportunity was there, and you could learn anything that you wanted to."[21]

Some CCC men used their leisure time to pursue journalism and work for the camp newspaper. The paper's staff came from those enrolled in the evening journalism classes held at the camp. Editor Joseph Stahl held to strict journalistic standards, ran short news stories about happenings at the camp and surrounding areas, and also included poetry, an editorial column, an occasional advice column, and every now and then a humorous story for balance. Contributors to *The Kendallite* were also eligible to have their stories picked up for publication in the national CCC newspaper, *Happy Days*. This opportunity provided an outlet for many aspiring journalists in the CCC, some of whom found positions with local papers or other New Deal programs such as the Federal Theater Project or the Federal Writer's Project after their tenure in the Corps had ended.[22]

But camp recreational opportunities only went so far. After forty hours of work and living on site, many enrollees wanted to get away and spend their leisure time in the towns and cities surrounding the camp. In turn, the surrounding towns were often grateful to have the CCC men visit for their spending provided a boost to the local economy. If the enrollees at the Kendall Reserve wanted to leave the camp to travel, the flatbed trucks normally used to transport workers to job sites functioned as buses, taking off with eight to ten men and stopping in Peninsula or Akron. As Peninsula was closer, the men would spend several hours in town on the weekends patronizing the local taverns or attending events such as motorcycle climbs that were within walking distance of the camp. This proximity came in handy if an enrollee got a little too carried away at the local bar. Friday and Saturday nights also held the possibility of dances in the small town, where young CCC men could get to know the local young ladies. Sometimes, the camp commander would invite women from Peninsula up to the camp for one of the Corps's four or five dances held throughout the year to commemorate the arrival of new enrollees, holidays, or other special occasions. These on-site dances allowed the camp leaders to monitor the activities of their boys and to prevent any scandalous behavior between them and the local girls.[23]

Akron was a popular destination for enrollees looking for a bigger-city experience with a bit more excitement than motorcycle climbs and small-town dances. Enrollee Tulloch said that oftentimes CCC boys would go to Akron to enjoy a good night of drinking and shenanigans "killing the mayor." He did not elaborate on what this was,

VKR truck accident, 1936 (National Park Service)

however. While this joke was probably harmless, enrollees occasionally did cause trouble after too many drinks in the Akron nightclubs. Enrollee Bereznak recalled one such instance involving him and four other enrollees. A young woman approached asking them to buy her a drink, a gesture they agreed to out of gentlemanly courtesy. She then asked the CCC men to buy her a flower, a move the men refused since they had little spending money and did not wish to spend it on something so frivolous. The girl complained to the club manager and a brawl broke out between the manager, his two bouncers, and the CCC group.

The next morning during roll call, the manager showed up at the camp with the Akron police looking to arrest the CCC members for their role in the melee. Bereznak noted that the camp captain defended the group, even going as far as making up a false night watch shift that the men were supposedly at instead of at the club and forcing the police off the camp premises. Despite whatever discipline the group faced from their Corps leaders, the CCC took measures to protect their boys from outside authority, knowing that in the end they were only young men looking for a good time away from the rigors of camp life. Camp officials also wanted to keep their CCC boys out of trouble for the simple fact that they were representatives of both the United States government and the New Deal and any infractions, however minor, would paint the entire organization in a negative light with the local communities.[24]

Occasionally enrollees traveled beyond Akron or Peninsula for a trip home to visit family. At most CCC camps across the country, leave provisions were typically generous and, provided that travel distance was not too far, many enrollees could go home to visit once a month if they desired. The men also got off for several holidays, including Christmas, Thanksgiving, and Easter, as well as three days off to go home to vote, and a week's vacation between service contracts. At Virginia Kendall, it was especially easy to take advantage of the leave policy since most of the men at the camp came from the Cleveland area. Enrollees were free to go home on the weekends after the final work shift ended at 4:30 P.M. on Friday afternoon and could stay as late as roll call on Monday morning. However, according to enrollee Tulloch, not all enrollees went home because they did not want to spend the ten-dollar round-trip fare—two weeks' pay—on the Greyhound bus to travel to Cleveland.[25] And besides, for most of the enrollees, there were plenty of opportunities for entertainment in and around the camp and a new group of companions to hang around with. They were a cohort, unified by similar experiences, thoughts, anxieties, inside jokes, and environment.

The situation was more complex for African American enrollees. While there were none at the reserve, these enrollees nonetheless played a vital role in the success of the CCC project. Helen Walker's student interviews with some of Ohio's black enrollees reveals that many came away from the project with improved work skills and sense of pride and accomplishment like many in the white cohort. One recruit, Paul Smith, "came away [from the CCC] proud to have learned something constructive," which aided him in getting employment after his term of service. However, nearly all of the fifty-nine African Americans that the group interviewed complained of racism within the officer ranks and discrimination from fellow white recruits. Initially, the officers for the camps came from the military. Many of these came from southern states and had a hard time adjusting to leading black recruits. One particular officer in an Ohio camp, who was later removed due to complaints filed with the state office, called them "insulting and derogatory names" and treated them very poorly.[26]

This was not unusual, as the CCC's overall record regarding African American enrollees was spotted with inconsistencies and intransigence. The original act that had created the Corps contained language that specifically said no American should be discriminated against because of color, race, or creed, yet Director Fechner let it be known very quickly that blacks would constitute no more than ten percent of the total CCC to correspond with their percentages within the total American population. Administrators did not implement this quota system for any other ethnicity and since blacks faced higher unemployment and poverty rates, their percentage of the total CCC should have been higher. The Corps was not unique in this, as most New Deal programs created racial quotas to limit the number of participating African Americans, except for the Federal Emergency Relief Administration (FERA). The CCC often sent black recruits to segregated camps, mostly in distant national park camps, like the one in Libby, Montana. There, twenty-five African American young men from New York and New Jersey arrived in 1933 and 1934 and over the next two years dug firebreaks, planted trees, built trails—all the things other CCC camps did. Yet, unlike the white camps, the local community did not welcome them. They were sometimes called "hoodlums" and had run-ins with local law enforcement officials. Eventually, white camp supervisors sent home or gave dishonorable discharges to almost half of the black enrollees for refusing to obey orders or work. Situations like this encouraged Fechner to issue an order in late 1934 that required all black units to be employed in their home states, again, a policy not implemented for white enrollees.

The segregation continued, and by 1935 only six percent of the enrollees were African American. In response, Roosevelt issued a new order requiring that African Americans be given positions of leadership and that target quotas be met. He did not however, do anything to redress the rampant segregation, leaving the day-to-day operations to Fechner and his advisors, and it would not be until 1940 that black officers were finally put into leadership positions and then only for all-black units. While there was pressure to integrate the camps, the CCC moved slowly on this and allowed local custom to determine the situation. All told, more than 300,000 African Americans served in the CCC by 1940, yet very few served alongside whites and most often faced more resentment from local communities. Even so, most of those interviewed by Walker and her students spoke enthusiastically about their CCC experience, echoing white enrollee's comments that the experience taught them how to work, transformed them physically, made them better individuals, and taught them the values of sacrifice, planning, and organization.[27]

An important part of the CCC's goal was to keep young enrollees out of trouble and to teach them obedience, reason, and order. Every camp did this through the grueling days the boys spent in outdoor work, but also through educational programs, leisure activities, and camp rules and regulations. The educational programs offered vocational and academic courses. With boys spending more time with their noses in books or learning a trade, camp supervisors could rest easier. Still, enrollees spent what little free time they did have in Peninsula, Cleveland, and most often, Akron, usually carousing in local bars. Although some of these boys managed to get into trouble when out on the town, most partook in the variety of recreational activities at the camp. They played sports, read books, went to dances, heard live music, and listened to the radio. Even through leisure activities and taking evening classes, the Kendall Reserve boys learned valuable lessons in self-improvement, one of the CCC's greatest objectives.

Campers arrive at VKR, no date (National Park Service)

Walking Today

KENNETH J. BINDAS, DAVID BUSCH, ANDREA HAUSER,
AND LINDSEY CALDERWOOD

The Virginia Kendall Reserve (VKR) remains an integral place for natural and recreational activities for the citizenry of northeastern Ohio and beyond. But much has changed since the CCC ended in 1942. In the two decades that followed World War II, the communities south of Cleveland and north of Akron continued to expand, encroaching into the Cuyahoga Valley. The development of interstate highways linked burgeoning suburbs to the working cities. As these developments grew, some local residents began to fear that the relative quiet of the valley would be lost and the VKR, as well as other natural spaces, would be threatened. Beginning in the early 1960s, local residents began organizing to protect the area in and around the reserve and found the welcome support of John F. Seiberling, scion of the Goodyear and Seiberling rubber companies, a member of the Tri-County Regional Planning Commission, and Democratic Congressman from the 14th District from 1971–1987. Seiberling also wanted to save the area from continued development, and working with Republican Congressman Ralph Regula of the 16th District and others, he lobbied President Gerald Ford in late 1974 to sign a bill designating the area as the Cuyahoga Valley National Recreation Area. Virginia Kendall remained a state park until 1978 when it was transferred to the National Park Service.

It would take the efforts of both men over the next three decades, however, to actually bring about the necessary infrastructure improvements, such as rehabilitating the Ohio-Erie towpath from Cleveland to Canal Fulton and beyond for bikers, runners, walkers, and hikers, and building visitors and environmental education centers and other facilities. The Cuyahoga River and the defunct Ohio-Erie canal corridor between Akron and Cleveland, had busy roadways on each side and were well travelled over the years, and debris, large and small, polluted some of the overgrown and neglected areas in between. Concerned citizens, with the sometimes reluctant cooperation of local, state, and federal officials, joined with volunteers and park service employees to reclaim neglected areas and clean up the garbage that blighted the area. In 2000, Representative Regula finally saw the fruits of his long battle with the region's designation changed to the Cuyahoga Valley National Park (CVNP). At that same time, the CCC legacy organization, made up of former members, their families, and others, placed Statue #8 (of fifty-four around the country) at the Happy Days visitor center. The son-in-law of former CCC boy Charles Varro (who was not assigned to this particular camp) paid for the installation, which, according to the organization, "stand[s] as a testament to the pride, hard work, and desire to teach the meaning of the CCC in America."[1]

CVNP employees, along with local volunteers, began to remake the region into a more usable recreational area by reclaiming the old canal towpath for hikers and bikers. The route begins at Lake Erie and Cleveland and will eventually connect all the way to New Philadelphia (encompassing more than 100 miles). Other natural attractions were developed and connected by trails within the park, including two ski resorts, Brandywine and Boston Mills, and a number of scenic waterfalls and bird-watching meadows. The CVNP now attracts more than two and half million visitors a year and ranks 30th in popularity of the 363 national parks. The area carved out by the CCC, the Virginia Kendall Reserve, remains one of the more popular destinations for hikers and picnickers. The Ledges area inspires and amazes young and old alike, and the facilities at the Octagon, Kendall Lake, the Ledges, and Happy Days continue to draw heavy use. The work done by the CCC boys has proved resilient to this traffic, remaining very close to its original look, although when something needs repair, the NPS has a difficult time matching the craftsmanship of the CCC work.

Kendall Lake, 1940s (National Park Service)

While the lake no longer invites swimmers and the toboggan run has long been closed, Kendall Lake remains very popular in all seasons. During the warmer seasons it is an excellent location to hike and feel the peacefulness of nature. In the winter, many residents follow the advice of park ranger Jennie Vasarhelyi to "get out and enjoy the natural wonder" with loved ones. "There is nothing quite like the thrill of speeding down the [Virginia Kendall] hills on a sled," she writes, where one can enjoy the "natural diversity" and bear witness to the "remarkable setting" of the region designed and created by the CCC. Echoing the sentiments of Harold S. Wagner from seventy-five years before, enjoying the Kendall Hills area should be an "escape from your everyday life into the rush of speed, the inspiration of spectacular views, [and] the wonder of nature."[2]

The story of the VKR is one that was replicated throughout the United States. Throughout the existence of the CCC, young workers revitalized and improved the lands in state and national parks, as well as national forests and other public lands.

Toboggan run, 1940s (National Park Service)

At Grand Canyon National Park in Arizona, for example, camps were set up at the bottom of the canyon and along the north and south rims. Aside from building shelters, rest houses, and stonewalls for safety, the CCC members constructed trails, roads and trans-canyon telephone lines.[3] The CCC also broke ground for and completed two-thirds of the 469-mile-long Blue Ridge Parkway spanning from Virginia's Skyline Drive through the Great Smoky Mountains of North Carolina. The project connected two national parks and promoted the development of lodges, restaurants, and numerous recreation areas for camping, swimming, and hiking.[4]

These are but two of hundreds of projects the CCC was involved in throughout the lower forty-eight states. When, in June 1935, Director Fechner issued a summary report describing the CCC's accomplishments over the previous two years, he claimed that CCC projects had assisted in developing, protecting, and perpetuating natural areas, in protecting and preserving wildlife, in restoring battlefield sites, in providing guide service, and in developing various facilities that provided the means to access and utilize scenic and primitive areas without despoiling them. A few of the projects he described included erosion work, spreading seed and sod over the grounds at Vicksburg

Toboggan run today (photo by Marina Vladova)

Icicles on the Octagon (photo by Marina Vladova)

National Military Park in Mississippi, and the restoration of national historic sites such as the Civil War battlefields outside Richmond, Virginia, and in places like Jamestown, Virginia, and Morristown, New Jersey. Other notable achievements included the construction of the Boulder City airport in Nevada, and the dams at Montgomery Bell, Tennessee, and Swift Creek, Virginia. Along with building trails and facilities, CCC members aided archaeologists in stabilizing the ancestral Pueblo sites at Bandelier National Monument in New Mexico and provided the labor for the pavement and enlargement of the underground rooms at Carlsbad Caverns National Park, also in New Mexico.[5]

The work of the CCC played a prominent role in creating the scenic face of America. There are hundreds of camps not as famous as those listed above whose work has had a long-term positive economic impact on the surrounding communities by continuing to draw people to the wonders of nature. For example, the swinging bridge, restroom facilities, trails, and roadways at Riverside State Park in Nine Mile Falls, Washington, provided hundreds of men with jobs during the Depression and provides a pleasurable recreation experience for nature seekers today.[6] One of the large log cabins built by the CCC in 1934 at Cook Forest State Park in Pennsylvania is now the Cook Forest Learning Center, which displays taxidermy animals and historic logging tools for public educational purposes.[7] One can search any state in the union for CCC parks and be astounded at the profundity of CCC activity across the country. This book is a tribute to all the CCC workers who worked to build better communities by working at camps like the Virginia Kendall Reserve.[8]

But what of the VKR today? How do people in the area use the natural environs that were so carefully crafted by the CCC boys? Several of us went to VKR in the spring of 2011 to talk with visitors, asking why they chose to visit and finding out if they knew anything about how the reserve came to be. By and large, we discovered that many people still utilize and appreciate the trails, trees, bridges, shelters, and lake that the CCC created during the 1930s, but they had little knowledge of who or what the CCC was. Mostly they agreed with Joe Kaser, a student hiking the trails with friends after they had finished finals at Kent State University and the University of Akron, respectively, who said, "there is so much to explore. I really love to come here and see nature."[9]

Flora at VKR (photo by Marina Vladova)

Pulling into any of the parking lots that ring the reserve one gets a sense of its popularity. When I visited on a cold, rainy Saturday morning in mid-May, the Ledges parking lot was already half full. Looking around at the people congregating and moving through the lot, some were dressed in running clothes and were obviously there to run the trails, while others were dressed in regular clothes with children in tow to walk the trails along the Ledges area, with its huge stone outcroppings.

Most people who come to the reserve do so for the hiking. The chance to walk through what they perceive to be unspoiled nature— "to get away from concrete," as one young hiker put it—allows people to experience the peace and quiet of this natural area, which is so close to highways, shopping areas, and cities. One woman named Kim echoed what many said when responding to the question why she makes the drive to the VKR: "because it's beautiful." She and her friend Tim drive for more than an hour from Sandusky several times a month to walk and run the many quiet trails throughout. "I think this whole area, this park [and surrounding CVNP area] are great, almost shocking," Kim said, because of its proximity to Cleveland and Akron. Another woman, unloading her car with picnic and party goods, was having her daughter's first birthday party at the Ledges shelter. She has come to the VKR since she was in high school growing up in west Akron, "going hiking (and) to hang out after school [enjoying] all the trails around it."

Then, an extended family—grandmother Shell, mother Shannon, with her daughter and son—arrived to begin a hike through the Ledges after a lunch at a local Burger King. The six-year-old, Jaden, explained that he likes to hike the trails while his older sister Cassandra just likes the quiet and nature. The family travels regularly from Kent to hike throughout the CVNP, but they have a special reverence for the VKR, especially Icebox Cave.[10]

Another family—Tim, Erica, and Chase from Stow, Ohio—also hikes the Ledges area "quite a bit." Ten-year-old Erica particularly likes the Icebox Cave area. Her father, Tim, uses the hikes to teach his children about nature and to appreciate the natural beauty of the area. "There was two cliffs and we saw a little hole and we walked through it to get back to the path," said Erica excitedly. She knew quite a bit about the history of the area, pointing out that the steps

Facing page: Hiking area near the Ice Box Cave (photo by Marina Vladova)

Light in the forest (photo by Marina Vladova)

were carved by "people," to which the father adds they had read the historical placard at the base to understand what it was they were experiencing. Tim explained that he talked to the kids about the CCC and its contribution of planting trees not just in VKR, but throughout the state. They also come in the wintertime to ride sleds down Kendall Hill by the lake. "Once they get a little older I'll have them start looking for salamanders," said Tim. Erica rubbed her hands and "ooohed" anticipating the hunt. On this day, they a saw a wild turkey and a pileated woodpecker—"you don't get to see one of those every day," said Tim. At one point while walking, Erica saw a ledge near the path and "there was no way to get down, and I jumped down." Her smile told of her joy.[11]

"This is my favorite spot, I love the rocks," said eighth-grade science teacher Betty. She considers herself something of a geological expert about the VKR, explaining that as part of her school's annual fundraising efforts, she auctions off a "guided hike" of the area detailing the geological history of the Ledges, as well as pointing out some of the interesting flora. She also regularly brings her students out to the reserve, showing them how a glacier tens of thousands of years ago had carved out the area, and other features, because there

Winter near the Octagon (photo by Marina Vladova)

is "lots to talk about." She also liked the park for its "micro-climate variety," making it an "unusual ecosystem in this area." It was clear from the conversation that she believed the area had been fairly wild forever and that the trees and brush were indigenous, at least since the glaciers had retreated. She knew that VKR used to be a state park but was surprised to learn the comprehensive role the CCC played in planting the trees, constructing the trails, and building the shelters.[12]

Betty's less than clear understanding of the historical context for VKR's creation was not unusual. Almost no one knew of the historical legacy of the reserve. Several mentioned they had seen and read the markers, which tell some of the story and are scattered around the trails, shelters, and lake, but by and large, most thought either that the area had always been a natural preserve or was just a wilderness. Kim and Paul, who travel from Sandusky to run the trails, had no idea of the CCC's role in the park.

They just enjoy this wonderful natural and free resource. Mike Vlasko, another athlete utilizing the trails for training—he's an active climber and runner—loves the area for its cleanliness and privacy. When asked about the area's history, he referred to the creation of the CVNP in the 1970s and '80s, but had little knowledge of what came before, saying, "I don't know much about the Virginia Kendall portion of" the CVNP. After I provided a basic outline of its creation, he remembered the placard near the stone steps carved out by the CCC and said he likes to look at it and see "what it looks like now compared to then." Virtually everyone we interviewed conformed to this narrative by first declaring their love of the area, the trails and its beauty, but then coming up short when discussing how it all came to be; none knew that most of the flora and fauna that had come to define the area came about largely as a result of the work done by the CCC boys.[13]

David Busch, one of the student authors, provides his own personal account. He grew up in the area and lived within walking distance of the reserve and it played a daily role in his life. He writes about one such recent visit when he interviewed visitors:

> There was still a gray overhang from the last night's rainstorm. Spring in Ohio turned out to be November slush. But the birds were chirping and soon, I hoped, summer would soon be here. I live on Truxell/Kendall Park Road, the old tree-logging road of Mr. Kendall himself. I often

Facing page: The Ledges in the fall (photo by Marina Vladova)

take my dog for a walk through Kendall Park and breathe the history with each step. I should interview myself, I thought, as I pulled out of my drive to meander down to Ledges Park. As I drove, I thought about the view from the Ledges and how it kindly embraces the Cuyahoga Valley; I thought about the young men in the Civilian Conservation Corps and their backbreaking yet meaningful work; and I thought of the meditative escape that the park has become for me. Do others relate to this park as I do? Or does each create their own relationship with the park? I think the latter and click my pen to go talk to the visitors of Kendall Park.

I first encounter two middle-aged men trudging from the north. One donned a fly hat, a fleece, and some hiking boots. "He's an avid hiker," I think as I cautiously walk up. The other one is in casual clothes: Khakis, t-shirt, and tennis shoes. I introduce myself and I ask them what brings them to the park. "Bird watching," the professional-looking hiker says. "We found 37 different species today," chirps in the other, with a proud smirk across his face. Eighty years ago birds would have had nowhere to land—Mr. Kendall was busy making money off of the tree line. Both seem truly interested in the conversation and I ask them what keeps bringing them back to the park. The avid hiker, who comes on a weekly basis, says it is mental therapy for him; cold or warm.

Cherry tree, Kendall Lake (photo by Marina Vladova)

Ledges adventure (photo by Marina Vladova)

The other tries to come twice a month and even more during the warm season. They were both from the Akron area and took a keen interest in the process of the book. "It is important to know the history of this park," the avid hiker says, "It's a treasure in your backyard." When Ken walked up, the other guy seemed to perk up a little more and the conversation turned political. In a fashion that was hard to follow at first, he asked my professor what the future of the park holds, especially if the park were to be privatized. That is the question of the future and the debate of the present, Ken responds. I nod. I hope politics does not destroy the work of the past and the gift of the present, I think as the conversation comes to an end.

As we split apart, I notice a Chevy Suburban roll confidently into the parking lot. The driver is smoking a cigarette and Ken turns to me and says, "I wonder what he'll do with the cigarette butt." I walk over to his car and as I begin to start the conversation, he defiantly responds that he is not interested in surveys. But, I tell him, I am a student from Kent State collaboratively writing a book on Kendall Park. His rude defense quickly dissipates. "Ask away," he responds in his raspy voice. He tells me that he enjoys coming to the Ledges often because of the unique Ice Box Cave. He enjoys quiet walks by himself, perhaps similar to the "mental therapy" of the other hiker. I ask if he knows much about the history behind the park and he says no. As I start to go into detail, I notice he pinches out his cigarette and throws it away in his car. I am glad for his respect for the park. He seems to be only partly interested in the conversation because his eyes and hands feverishly work his iPhone. I would find out that he was mapping out his route for the day. "I don't need the trails," he explains, "too many people on the trails." Our conversation quickly comes to an end and as I turn to go he tells me that Kendall Park is the "Jewel of all the Parks." Thank the CCC, I think to myself as I walk away. As I approach Ken, I take a deep breath and hear a robin call in the distance. I wonder what Mr. Kendall would think today. I wonder what the CCC would think today. Perhaps it doesn't matter. Perhaps what matters is what they have provided for the American visitor in the twenty-first century.

Path leading to the Ledges from Happy Days (photo by Marina Vladova)

A place for reflection (photo by Marina Vladova)

That last thought became especially true as I walked up to a young father and his daughter. He was from Fairlawn, Ohio, and took a hesitant interest in my questions and the book. He didn't know much about the park and as I began to explain, his attention was fully encompassed by his young daughter. "I come here to escape the world," he tells me but "mostly I come here for the kids." I smile and I quickly understand that he wants to be alone with his daughter. "Want me to skip the rock?" the father asks his young daughter as I walk away. As I heard the rock splash across the surface of Kendall Lake, I thought about Red Adams and William Reed, young CCC workers from Camp 576, who sweated, laughed, and worked their soul into this lake. And so Hugh Wagner was right. Visitors today should be everlastingly grateful for the work done by the CCC.

Notes

Introduction

1. For an excellent overview, see Virginia Kendall Reserve State Park Historic District, National Register of Historical Places Registration Form, U.S. Department of the Interior, prepared by Jeffrey Winstel, National Park Service, 1995, section E, Statement of Historic Context, hereafter referred to as NRHP; Ron Cockrell, *A Green Shrouded Miracle: The Administrative History of Cuyahoga Valley National Recreation Area* (Omaha, Nebraska: U.S. Department of the Interior, NPS, 1992), Chapter 1, "A Brief History of the Cuyahoga Valley"; Carolyn V. Platt, *Cuyahoga Valley National Park Handbook* (Kent, Ohio: Kent State University Press, in cooperation with Cuyahoga Valley National Park, 2006), 9–15.

1. The CCC Comes to Virginia Kendall Reserve

1. Akron, Ohio: WADC, March 5, 1939.

2. Virginia Kendall Reserve State Park Historic District, National Register of Historical Places Registration Form, U.S. Department of the Interior, prepared by Jeffrey Winstel, National Park Service, 1995, 29, hereafter referred to as NRHP; Narrative Report of CCC Accomplishments, submitted by Forrest E. Smith, Project Supervisor for Ohio S.P. 5, CCC Co. 576, Peninsula, Summit County, Ohio, page 1, in CCC Reports, 1935–1936, CVVA 15294, container #3, folder #12, Cuyahoga Valley National Park Archives, hereafter referred to as CCC Reports, 1935–36; Franklin D. Roosevelt, "As the President Sees It," in *The New America: The Spirit of the Civilian Conservation Corps,* by Alfred C. Oliver and Harold M. Dudley (New York: Longmans, Green and Co., 1937), xix.

3. Harold T. Pinkett, *Preliminary Inventory of the Records of the Civilian Conservation Corps* (Washington, D.C.: National Archives, 1948), 1–3.

4. John C. Paige, "The Civilian Conservation Corps and the National Park Service, 1933–1945: An Administrative History," National Park Service, U.S. Department of the Interior study (Washington D.C.: Government Printing Office, 1985), 9–34; Elden B. Sessions, "Educational Work of the Civilian Conservation

Corps Camps in Ohio," unpublished dissertation, Ohio State University, 1937, pages 1–10; Stanley Cohen, *The Tree Army: A Pictorial History of the Civilian Conservation Corps, 1933–1942* (Missoula, Montana: Pictorial Histories Publishing Company, 1980), 6–15; Robert Fechner, "A Short Story of the CCC," in *The New America,* 19–28. Quotes from pages 23, 24, and 28.

5. *Annual Report of the Civilian Conservation Corps: Fiscal Year Ended June 30, 1938* (Washington, D.C.: Government Printing Office, 1938), numbers taken from pages 5–11, 91–95.

6. Sessions, 28–40; NRHP, 34–36; *Annual Report, 1938,* 85–103.

7. Arthur Dunham, "Building Men—Growing Trees," *The Survey* 69 (May 1933): 187; Franklin D. Roosevelt, March 9, 1933, speech, http://www.presidency. ucsb.edu/franklin_roosevelt.php; Phoebe Cutler, *The Public Landscape of the New Deal* (New Haven: Yale University Press, 1985), 66; NRHP, quote from pages 41–42.

8. Franklin D. Roosevelt, "As the President Sees It," in *The New America: The Spirit of the Civilian Conservation Corps,* by Alfred C. Oliver and Harold M. Dudley (New York: Longmans, Green and Co., 1937), xix; "Asks More Parks," editorial, Cleveland *Plain Dealer,* July 5, 1936, 18:2; Fanning Hearon, "The Recreation Renaissance," *Recreation* 29 (September 1935): 289–93, quotes from pages 289 and 293; William Welcome Wills, "C.C.C. Stone and Log Craft," *Industrial Education* 39 (November 1937): 250–53.

9. Neil M. Maher, *Nature's New Deal: The Civilian Conservation Corps and the Roots of the American Environmental Movement* (New York: Oxford University Press, 2008), 21; A. L. Riesch Owen, *Conservation Under FDR* (New York: Praeger Publishers, 1983), 5; Harold T. Pinkett, *Gifford Pinchot: Private and Public Forester* (Urbana, Ill.: University of Illinois Press, 1970), 150.

10. Samuel P. Hays, *The Response to Industrialism, 1885–1914* (Chicago: The University of Chicago Press, 1957), 88–89.

11. Neil Maher, "A New Deal Body Politic: Landscape, Labor, and the Civilian Conservation Corps," *Environmental History* 7, no. 3 (July 2002): 450.

12. T. J. Jackson Lears, *No Place of Grace: Antimodernism and the Transformation of American Culture, 1880–1920* (New York: Pantheon Books, 1981), 90.

13. NRHP, 27–47. Quote from page 32.

14. Susan V. Garland, The Civilian Conservation Corps in the Cuyahoga Valley Oral History Project (CUVA 15294 Container 3 Folder 24), 6–8.

15. Davis and Ulrich quoted in "The Inquiring Reporter," *Akron Beacon Journal,* March 10, 1942; "County Enriched $750,000 By CCC," *Akron Beacon Journal,* April 4, 1939.

16. CCC Reports, 1935–1936, March 31, 1936, brief resume as prepared for Mr. McKinney; *The Kendallite,* January 31, 1936, Joseph Stahl, 2; *The Kendallite,* CCC camp, August 2, 1935, page 12; *Ridge Runners' Record* (camp newspaper when the CCC was transferred to Sand Run Park in 1937), June 1937, 2, editorials.

17. Wagner to G. C. Harman, inspector, second district, State Park Emergency Conservation Work office, January 31, 1934; Wagner to Harman, January 11, 1934, both Wagner Letters, CVVA; Joseph Stahl, "A Brief History of the Virginia Kendall State Park," *The Kendallite,* January 17, 1936, 2.

18. Wagner to Harmon, June 14, 1935; Wagner to Herbert Evison, regional officer, Region One, Branch of Planning and State Cooperation, Attn: K. C. Mc-Carter, technical coordinator, September 18, 1936, Wagner Letters, CVVA.

19. Wagner to Evison, September 19, 1936, Wagner Letters, CVVA. Leonard Tulloch, interviewed by Susan Garland, July, 1979, Cuyahoga National Park oral history project, park archives, pages 16–17, hereafter referred to as Name, CVNP oral history, page number.

20. Wagner to R. F. Wirsching, inspector, District D—Region One, Branch of Planning and State Cooperation, NPS, February, 19, 1937; Joseph Stahl, "A Brief History of the Virginia Kendall Reserve," *The Kendallite*, January 31, 1936, 2, Wagner Letters, CVVA; Wagner to Conrad L. Wirth, Supervisor of Recreation and Land Planning, NPS, U.S. Department of the Interior, August 30, 1938, Wagner Letters, CVVA.

21. NRHP, 28–29; Mick Skrattish, *Historic Resource Study: The Cuyahoga Valley National Recreation Area* (Denver: Department of the Interior, NPS, 1985), 240–42; Wagner to NPS, September 9, 1938; Wagner to Conrad L. Wirth, February 4, 1936; Wagner to Herbert Evison, associate regional director, Region One, NPS, June 23, 1938; Wagner to Wirshing, February 19, 1937, CVVA; Tulloch, CVNP oral history, 3.

22. NRHP, 29–30.

2. Work Builds Better Men

1. Letter from A. H. Good to Wagner, February 14, 1934. H. S. Wagner, NPS Copies of Correspondence related to CCC, 1934–1942. CVVA 15294, Container #3, Folder #21. Hereafter referred to as Wagner Letters, CVVA.

2. *Annual Report, 1938*, 70–72; Elden B. Sessions, "Educational Work of the Civilian Conservation Corps Camps in Ohio," PhD diss., The Ohio State University, 1937, 41–58. Sessions also asked the 600 their future vocational expectations and while nearly half chose "uncertain," a majority of those who picked an occupation selected mechanic, factory worker, clerk, famer, trucker, or welder. See Sessions, page 63.

3. Helen M. Walker, *The CCC Through the Eyes of 272 Boys: A Summary of a Group Study of the Reactions of 272 Cleveland Boys to Their Experience in the Civilian Conservation Corps* (Cleveland: Western Reserve University Press, 1938), 7–25. Much of what Walker writes about the generational division within the families of enrollees is similar to Lizabeth Cohen's *Making a New Deal: Industrial Workers in Chicago, 1919–1939* (New York: Cambridge University Press, 1990, 2008), especially pages 53–98; Ralph Kelly, "Foresters Speeded to Fort Know: Esprit de Corps Develops Among 324 Recruits on Train," Cleveland *Plain Dealer* April 12, 1933, 1:2.

4. Roosevelt quote from *Reforestation by the CCC* (Washington, D.C: Government Printing Office, 1941), 13; Maher, *Nature's New Deal*, 6; editorial, *The Kendallite*, August 30, 1935, 1–2; Leonard H. Tulloch, CCC, oral history, August 23, 1980, CUVA 15294, container 1, folder 2, page 6.

5. CCC camp newspaper, *The Kendallite,* May 25, 1937, editorial, "Memories," 2; Leonard H. Tulloch, CCC, oral history, August 23, 1980, CUVA 15294, container 1, folder 2, page 6; "No Pork Barrel," Cleveland *Plain Dealer,* December 4, 1936, 10:1.

6. James Wilson, "Community, Civility, and Citizenship: Theatre and Indoctrination in the Civilian Conservation Corps of the 1930s," *Theatre History Studies* 23 (June, 2003), quote from page 77; the whole article is a valuable discussion of the role and influence of theater on the unity and success of the CCC; *The CCC at Work: A Story of 2,500,000 Young Men* (Washington, D.C.: FSA/CCC, 1941), 94, 102.

7. Walker, *The CCC,* 46–50; Captain A. W. Belden, "Editorial," *The Kendallite,* July 19, 1935, 2; Wagner, letter to G. C. Harman, inspector, second district, March 6, 1934, CVNP archives.

8. Maher, *Nature's New Deal,* quotes, in order, pages 96, 93, and 83. See pages 77–113. Jeffrey Ryan Suzik, "Building Better Men: The CCC Boy and the Changing Social Ideal of Manliness," *Men and Masculinity* 2 (October, 1999): 152–79. Quote from page 166.

9. Christopher Wilk, "The Healthy Body Culture," in *Modernism: Designing a New World, 1914–1939* (London: V & A Publications, 2006), 249–96. Quote from page 250.

10. Walker, *The CCC,* 29–31, 81–83.

11. Roosevelt, A Radio Address on the Third Anniversary of the CCC, April 17, 1936, *The Public Papers and Addresses of Franklin D. Roosevelt,* vol. 5 (New York: Random House, 1938), 170; NPS, page 33; Tulloch oral history, pages 6, 33–34; "Editorial," *The Kendallite,* August 30, 1935, 2; Robert Fechner, frontispiece, *CCC in Ohio* (Columbus, Ohio: Federal Writers Project Publication, 1938), 1.

12. Tulloch oral history, pages 6 and 8; Walker, The CCC, 36.

13. Tulloch oral history, August 23, 1980, CUVA 15294, container 1, folder 2, page 25; Walker, *The CCC,* 32.

14. *The Kendallite,* August 30, 1935, 2; CCC newspaper, *Ridge Runners' Record,* June 1937, 2, editorials; Walker, *The CCC,* 32.

15. Suzik, "Building Better Men"; *The Kendallite,* August 30, 1935, 4.

16. Edwin T. Randall, "CCC Host Building Up Ohio's Forests: 36,000 Boys in 18 Camps are Planting Trees, Making Roads, and Saving Soil," Cleveland *Plain Dealer* August 6, 1933, C8:8+; "Local Boys in Camp," letter to the editor from Stanley A. Zabawski and Louis Zarnowski, Cleveland *Plain Dealer,* July 8, 1934, A17:1; Terry Montaquila, August 19, 1981, CUVA 15294, container 1, folder 2, page 9; for an early romantic interpretation of the regenerative powers of nature via the CCC, see Walter Davenport, "Thy Woods and Templed Hills," *Collier's* 92 (September 9, 1933): 10–12, 31.

17. A. W. Bolden, *The Kendallite,* July 19, 1935, editorial.

18. John B. Derden, "The Biography of John B. Derden: CCC Man, Company 3435, Camp P-87, Rome, Georgia, and Company 5463, Camps F-41, Ruch, Oregon," from *The Justin Museum* 7 <http://www.justinmuseum.com/oralbio/derdenbio .html> (accessed 11/30/2009).

19. Basic information on CCC camp setup and daily function was pulled from several sources, including: Maher, *Nature's New Deal,* 77–113; Joseph M.

Speakman, "Into the Woods: The First Year of the Civilian Conservation Corps," *The U.S. National Archives and Records Administration* 38, no. 3 (2006): 1–11; John A. Salmond, *The Civilian Conservation Corps 1933–1942: A New Deal Case Study* (Durham, N.C.: Duke University Press, 1967); Joan Sharpe, "Uncle Sam and the CCC," *World War II Journal—WWII Remembrance Week,* 2006 <http://www.ccclegacy.org/uncle_sam_&_ccc.htm> (accessed 11/30/2009); Helen M. Walker, *The CCC Through the Eyes of the 272 Boys* (Cleveland, Ohio: Western Reserve University Press, 1938); references to the camps being efficient networks of control come from ideas expressed in Terry Smith's *Making the Modern: Industry, Art, and Design in America* (Chicago: The University of Chicago Press, 1993).

20. For more information about why the army was charged with the running of the camps, see Patel, 163–64; Jennifer D. Keene, *Doughboys, the Great War, and the Remaking of America* (Baltimore: The Johns Hopkins University Press, 2001), 36–42; Sessions, "Educational Work," 176; Maher, *Nature's New Deal*, 86; Speakman, "Into the Woods," 4.

21. James L. Fitzpatrick, "Conserving Forests and Rebuilding Men: The CCC As Part of the New Deal," *Scholastic* 24 (March 17, 1934): 23–25; Captain X, "A Civilian Army in the Woods," *Harper's Magazine* 168 (March 1934): 487–97.

22. Size of the 1933 army from: "American Military History," *Army Historical Series: Center of Military History* (Washington D.C.: United States Army, 1989) <http://www.history.army.mil/BOOKS/amh/amh-19.htm>, last modified 4/25/2001 (accessed 11/30/2009); Maher, 79–80.

23. Salmond, *A New Deal Case Study,* 177–79; Maher, 83–107; Speakman, "Into the Woods," 4

24. Unknown, "Barrack Enrollee Adams is Buried," *The Kendallite,* July 19, 1935; unknown, "Drowning Rabbit Is Rescued," *The Kendallite,* September 27, 1935; Susan V. Garland, interview with Paul Tulloch, Cuyahoga Valley National Recreation Area, July 1979.

25. Maher, 93–96

26. CCC Handbook, Introduction <http://www.justinmuseum.com/cccpapers/handbk1.jpg> (accessed on 11/30/2009). Note: there is no date on the handbook itself. From reading through the sections of the pamphlet available online, it seems to have been issued after 1935.

27. Education quote from Maher, 86, 163–64.

28. Susan V. Garland, "The Civilian Conservation Corps in the Cuyahoga Valley," research paper, Cuyahoga Valley Archives, 1979, pages 16–20; typescript radio interview, WADC, March 3, 1939, VKR CCC Records, Akron Public Library, page 3; Harold S. Wagner, interview by Susan V. Garland, May 27, 1980, folder 3, container 1, CVVA 15294, Cuyahoga Valley Archives, Peninsula, Ohio; Maher, 84.

29. Walker, *The CCC,* 38, 42, and 67; Harold S. Wagner, interview by Susan V. Garland, October 22, 1979, folder 14, container 1, CVVA 15294, Cuyahoga Valley Archives, Peninsula, Ohio; Leonard H. Tulloch, interview by Susan V. Garland, May 23, 1980, folder 2, container 1, CVVA 15294, Cuyahoga Valley Archives, Peninsula, Ohio; Maher, 86; A. W. Belden, editorial, *The Kendallite,* July 19, 1935.

30. Floyd Bendik, Cuyahoga oral history interview. CVNP Oral history.

3. Creating Nature

1. Franklin D. Roosevelt, Executive Order 6101, Starting the Civilian Conservation Corps, April 5, 1933. From John T. Woolley and Gerhard Peters, *The American President Project* (online), University of California at Santa Barbara, Gerhard Peters (database) <http://www.presidency.ucsb.edu/ws/?pid=14609>; Franklin D. Roosevelt, "As the President Sees It," in *The New America: The Spirit of the Civilian Conservation Corps,* by Alfred C. Oliver and Harold M. Dudley (New York: Longmans, Green and Co., 1937), xix.

2. Franklin D. Roosevelt, March 9, 1933, speech; Phoebe Cutler, *The Public Landscape of the New Deal* (New Haven, Conn.: Yale University Press, 1985), 66; NRHP, quote from pages 41–42.

3. *Reforestation by the CCC* (Washington D.C.: GPO, 1941), quote from page 9; William C. Tweed, Laura E. Soulliere, and Henry G. Law, *National Park Service: Rustic Architecture, 1916–1942* (NPS Online Book <http://www.nps.gov/history/history/online_books/rusticarch/note.htm>), Section V. Roosevelt's Emergency Programs: 1933–1935, pages 1–13; Walter Rogers, *The Professional Practice of Landscape Architecture: A Complete Guide* (New York: John Wiley & Sons, 1997), 1–21.

4. Terry Smith, *Making the Modern: Industry, Art, and Design in America* (Chicago: University of Chicago Press, 1993), 12–77, quote from page 8; Albert H. Good, *Park and Recreation Structures* (New York: Princeton Architectural Press, 1999; a reprint of the 1938 edition published by the U.S. Department of the Interior, National Park Service), 5–8, quote from page 5. Wagner's recommendation of Good found in Wagner's letter to Ickes, December 1, 1933, as cited in Nick Scrattish, *Historic Resource Study: Cuyahoga Valley National Recreation Area* (Denver Service Center: U.S. Department of the Interior, National Park Service, 1985), 238 n. 92, 255.

5. Forrest E. Smith, superintendent, CCC unit #576, Narrative Report of CCC Accomplishments, March 31, 1936, listings. NPN. CCC Reports, 1935–36.

6. Sarah T. Phillips, *This Land, This Nation: Conservation, Rural America, and the New Deal* (New York: Cambridge University Press, 2007), provides an excellent discussion of the role and meaning of New Deal policies and their effect on the environment and the conservation movement, particularly pages 1–74. See also Tarlock, "Rediscovering the New Deal's Environmental Legacy," 155–76; quotes from NRHP, 45, 47; see also Linda Flint McClelland, *Building the National Parks: Historic Landscape Design and Construction* (Baltimore, Md.: The Johns Hopkins University Press, 1998), especially chapter 10, "A New Deal for State Parks," 381–424.

7. U.S. Department of the Interior, National Park Service, *National Register of Public Places,* by Jeffrey Winstel, NPS Form 10–900, Peninsula, Ohio, June 1995, 41.

8. Albert Good, quoted in Winstel, 30; Harold S. Wagner to R. F. Wirsching, February 19, 1937, Akron Metropolitan Park District, Akron, Ohio, 2.

9. Winstel, 50–54.

10. Christopher Green, "The Machine," in *Modernism: Designing a New World,* ed. Christopher Wilk (London: V&A Publications, 2006), 86; Tim Benton, "Modernism and Nature," also in *Modernism,* 311–40, quote from page 318.

11. Winstel, 44; Wagner to Wirsching, 2.

12. Winstel, 6; Wagner to Wirsching, 1.

13. Virginia Kendall State Park, Ohio S.P. 5 CCC Co. 576, *Narrative Report of C.C.C. Accomplishments*, by Forrest E. Smith (Peninsula, Ohio, March 31, 1936), 1–3.

14. Harold S. Wagner to Herbert Evison, September 18, 1938, Akron Metropolitan Park District, Akron, Ohio, 2.

15. Virginia Kendall State Park, Ohio S.P. 5 CCC Co. 576, *Draft: Brief resume as prepared for Mr. Kinney*, by Forrest E. Smith (Peninsula, Ohio, March 31, 1936), 1–2; U.S. War Department, "Participation of the War Department in the Emergency Conservation Work," In *Two Years of Emergency Conservation Work (Civilian Conservation Corps)*, excerpts from reports prepared by the War Department (March 1933–March 1935), 4, 2.

16. Walker, *The CCC*, 73.

17. Tulloch, oral history, 10–11; Maher, 54; Conrad Wirth, *Civilian Conservation Corps Program of the United States Department of the Interior*, March 1933 to June 30, 1943, a report to Harold L. Ickes, Secretary of the Interior, (Washington D.C.: Government Printing Office, January, 1944), 2–5.

4. Leisure Is Learning

1. Al Sommer, CCC Oral History, August 11, 1979, Thelma Smith, CUVA 15294, container 1, folder 47, page 12; Wagner, letter to G. C. Harman, inspector, second district, March 6, 1934, CVNP archives.

2. Clarence Rainwater, *The Play Movement in the United States* (Washington, D.C.: McGrath Publishing Company, 1922), 20–44.

3. Rainwater, *The Play Movement*, 54–69, 117.

4. Susan Currell, *The March of Spare Time: The Problem and Promise of Leisure* (Philadelphia, Pa.: University of Pennsyvalnia Press, 2005), 18–30, quote from page 30.

5. Edwin T. Randall, "Hard Work, Hard Play and Heaped Dinner Plates Have Replaced Idleness in Homes Supported by Charity, and These Men Love it," Cleveland *Plain Dealer* July 16, 1933, 1:1; "CCC Host Building Up Ohio's Forests," Cleveland *Plain Dealer*, C8:8.

6. "Letters to the Voice of Experience," *The Kendallite*, March 13, 1936, 4.

7. Elden B. Sessions, "Educational Work of the Civilian Conservation Corps Camps in Ohio," unpublished dissertation, Ohio State University, 1937, 158–60, 172–74, 196.

8. Leonard Tulloch, CVNP oral history, 33; "Enrollee Carline Killed in Accident," *The Kendallite*, May 8, 1936, 1; "Carl Korosech is Killed," *The Kendallite*, August 2, 1935, 1.

9. *A Manual for Instructors in the Civilian Conservation Corps Camps* (Washington, D.C.: Government Printing Office, 1935), 1–4, 51; Walker, *The CCC Through the Eyes of 272 Boys*, 37–43; "Educational Program Announced," *The Kendallite*, July 19, 1935, 1; Sessions, "Educational Work," 178–85, 236.

10. A. W. Bolden, editorial, *The Kendallite*, , July 19, 1935; John Hines, "Memories," *The Kendallite*, May 25, 1937; "Letters to Voice of In-experience," *The Kendal-*

lite, March 13, 1936; David Welky, *Everything Was Better in America: Print Culture in the Great Depression* (Chicago: University of Illinois Press, 2008), 215–17.

11. Joseph Stahl, editorial, *The Kendallite,* March 17, 1936.

12. Helen M. Walker, *The CCC Through the Eyes of 272 Boys: A Summary of a Group Study of the Reactions of 272 Cleveland Boys to Their Experience in the Civilian Conservation Corps* (Cleveland: Western Reserve University Press, 1938), 37–38.

13. Garland, 19–20; CCC Reunion, interview by Susan V. Garland, August 26, 1979, folder 1, container 1, CVVA 15294, Cuyahoga Valley Archives, Peninsula, Ohio; Walker, *The CCC,* 40.

14. "Visions CCC New Educational Tool," Cleveland *Plain Dealer* October 26, 6:2; *The Kendallite,* August 30, 1935, 2 (17); F. J. O'Leary, CCC, oral histories, Virginia Kendall Reserve, August 1, 1979, CUVA 15294, container 1, folder 19, page 15; *The Kendallite,* July 19, 1935; Maher, 90.

15. National Recreation Association, quoted in Sessions, 139–41.

16. John Salmond, *The Civilian Conservation Corps 1933–42: A New Deal Case Study* (Durham, N.C.: Duke University Press, 1967), 139, 142. Salmond gives a good overview of the corps across the entire United States and provides many examples that are also relevant for the Virginia Kendall Reserve; Sam Bereznak, interviewed by Susan Garland, December 4, 1980, at Cuyahoga Valley National Park, Cuyahoga Valley National Park Archives, CUVA 15291, container 1, folder 41, pages 21–22; "Baseball Season Closes for 576," *The Kendallite,* August 10, 1936, 1; "576 Joins Class A Basketball League," *The Kendallite,* January 17, 1936, 1.

17. "Educational Programs Announced," *The Kendallite,* July 19, 1935, 1. The boxing and wrestling classes were held Tuesday and Thursday nights at 6:30 and 8:30, respectively; Bereznak, 22; Francis O'Leary, interviewed by Susan Garland, August 1, 1979, at Cuyahoga Valley National Park, Cuyahoga Valley National Park Archives, CUVA 15291, container 1, folder 19, page 24.

18. Walker, *The CCC,* 47; "Eight-Balls Take Beatings as New Table Arrives," *The Kendallite,* August 10, 1936, 1; "Recreational Facilities Improved," *The Kendal-lite,* September 13, 1935, 1; and "Ceiling in Rec Hall is Replaced," *The Kendallite,* January 17, 1936, 1.

19. Tulloch, 30; "Barracks #3 has Entertainment," *The Kendallite,* July 19, 1935, 3; "WPA Colored Orchestra Entertains Co. 576," *The Kendallite,* August 10, 1936, 1. We found it interesting how the different New Deal programs interacted with one another. WPA theater projects also toured throughout CCC camps (although no record of a performance at Virginia Kendall could be found) and the WPA writers' project was charged with developing promotional pamphlets advertising and promoting the CCC in geographic areas.

20. "Educational Programs Announce," *The Kendallite,* July 19, 1935, 1; O'Leary, 28. Both elementary and advanced photography classes were offered on Monday nights at 6:30 and 8:30, respectively; Walker, *The CCC,* 73; Salmond, *A New Deal Case Study,* 139–40; "Library Receives 46 Books," *The Kendallite,* September 13, 1935, 1; Tulloch, 30; CCC oral history, F. J. O'Leary, August 1, 1979, CUVA 15294, container 1, folder 19, page 35.

21. Joseph Stahl, editorial, *The Kendallite,* July 19, 1935, 2; Salmond, *A New Deal Case Study,* 143.

22. Walker, *The CCC*, 49; CCC Reunion, 5–6.

23. Tulloch, 29. Tullolch does not clarify the meaning of this statement: whether this was a drunken joke or some CCC enrollee actually proposed to do such a deed, I do not know of any harm coming to Akron's leaders due to intoxicated corps enrollees; Bereznak, 18–21.

24. Salmond, *A New Deal Case Study*, 141; CCC Reunion, 4–5; Tulloch, 31.

25. Walker, *The CCC*, 50–53, 70–71.

26. Paige, "The Civilian Conservation Corps and the National Park Service," 93–95; Dwayne Mack, "May the Work I've Done Speak for Me: African American Civilian Corps Enrollees in Montana, 1933–1934," *The Western Journal of Black Studies* 27 (2003): 236–45; Walker, *The CCC*, 74–75, 88.

Conclusion: Walking Today

1. From <http://www.nps.gov/cuva/planyourvisit/upload/History7%20final.pdf> (accessed May 16, 2011); an excellent overview of the park is <http://openlibrary.org/books/OL1329130M/A_green_shrouded_miracle—addImage>; Ron Cockrell, *A Green Shrouded Miracle: The Administrative History of Cuyahoga Valley National Recreation Area, Ohio* (Omaha, Neb.: National Park Service, U.S. Dept. of the Interior, Midwest Regional Office, Office of Planning and Resource Preservation, Cultural Resources Management, 1992); statue program, no. 8, dedicated September 8, 2000, <http://www.ccclegacy.org> (accessed 5/4/11).

2. Jennie Vasarhelyi, "Discover Wintertime Fun at CVNP's Virginia Kendall Hills," *The Westside Leader*, January 25, 2007, at <http://www.akron.com/20070125/wsl69.asp> (accessed 5/4/11).

3. Robert Audretsch, *Grand Canyon Civilian Conservation Corps*, National Park Service, U.S. Department of Interior, last updated November 15, 2010, <http://www.nps.gov/grca/historyculture/ccc.htm>.

4. Tim Treadwell, *Blue Ridge Parkway and Skyline Drive*, Parkway History, <http://www.blueridgeskyline.com/history.php> (accessed March 25, 2011).

5. Harlan D. Unrau and G. Frank Williss, *Administrative History: Expansion of the National Park Service in the 1930s* (Denver Service Center: National Park Service, September 1983), <http://www.cr.nps.gov/history/online_books/unrau-williss/adhi3a.htm> (last modified March 14, 2000); Bandelier National Monument, *CCC Walking Tour Intro*, National Park Service, U.S. Department of Interior, <http://www.nps.gov/band/photosmultimedia/ccc-wt-vt-intro.htm> (last updated December 4, 2007).

6. Riverside State Park, *CCC at Riverside*, <http://www.riversidestatepark.org/ccc_at_riverside.htm> (accessed March 25, 2011).

7. *Cook Forest State Park*, Pennsylvania Department of Conservation and Natural Resources, <http://www.dcnr.state.pa.us/stateparks/parks/cookforest.aspx> (accessed March 25, 2011); Historical Points of Interest in Cook Forest, *Log Cabin Inn* (Cook Forest Online: 2010), <http://www.cookforest.com/activities/historic.cfm> (accessed March 25, 2011).

8. A selected list of articles include Carol Ahlgren, "The Civilian Conservation Corps and Wisconsin State Park Development," *Wisconsin Magazine of History* 71 (Spring 1988): 184–204; Patrick Clancy, "Conserving the Youth: The CCC Experience in the Shenandoah National Park," *Virginia Magazine of History and Biography* (Autumn 1997): 439–72; Peter M. Booth, "Cactizonians: The CCC in Pima County, 1933–1942," *Journal of Arizona History* 32 (Autumn 1991): 291–332; Kenneth Hendrickson, "Relief for Youth: The CCC and the NYA in North Dakota," *North Dakota History* 48, no. 4 (Fall, 1981): 17–27; Leo Kimmett, "Life in a Yellowstone CCC Camp," *Annals of Wyoming* 56 (Spring 1984): 12–21; Michael J. Ober, "The CCC Experience in Glacier National Park," *Montana, The Magazine of Western History* 26 (July 1976): 30–39; Roger Rosenstreet, "Roosevelt's Tree Army: The CCC in Michigan," *Michigan History* 70 (May–June 1986): 14–23; Jerrell H. Shofner, "Roosevelt's Tree Army: The CCC in Florida," *Florida Historical Quarterly* 65 (April 1987): 433–56; John J. Sullivan, "The CCC and the Creation of Myakka State Park," *Tampa Bay History* 9 (Winter 1987): 4–16; Robert A. Waller, "The CCC and the Emergence of South Carolina's State Park System, 1933–1942," *South Carolina Historical Magazine* 104 (April 2003): 101–25. There are more in smaller selected journals and newsletters. There are also a variety (in terms of quality and quantity) of books on state-wide CCC activity and can be easily searched via the web or by consulting Neil Maher's excellent overview of the project, *Nature's New Deal* (New York: Oxford University Press, 2007).

9. Joe Kaser was interviewed by Colleen Benoit and Michele Curran on May 12, 2011. Hereafter referred to as VKR interviews, subject name.

10. VKR interviews, C. J. Tromm; Joy, last name not given, interviewed by Ken Bindas, May 14, 2011. Hereafter, name, Bindas VKR; Jaden, Cassandra, Shell, and Shannon, no last names, Bindas VKR.

11. Tim, Erica, and Chase DeRossa, Bindas VKR.

12. Betty Indriolo, Bindas VKR.

13. Kim and Paul, Bindas VKR; Mike Vlasko, Bindas VKR; VKR interviews, Joe, Lily, and C. J. Tromm.

Index